César Chávez

THE OKLAHOMA WESTERN BIOGRAPHIES
RICHARD W. ETULAIN, GENERAL EDITOR

César Chávez with workers during Coachella strike, 1973.

César Chávez

A TRIUMPH OF SPIRIT

By Richard Griswold del Castillo and Richard A. Garcia

UNIVERSITY OF OKLAHOMA PRESS: NORMAN

Published with the assistance both of the National Endowment for the Humanities, a federal agency which supports the study of such fields as history, philosophy, literature, and language, and of the Andrew W. Mellon Foundation.

Library of Congress Cataloging-in-Publication Data

Griswold del Castillo, Richard.
    César Chávez : a triumph of spirit / by Richard Griswold del Castillo and Richard A. Garcia.
        p. cm. — (The Oklahoma western biographies : v. 11)
    Includes bibliographical references (p.   –   ) and index.
    ISBN: 0–8061–2758–9 (cloth : alk. paper)
    1. Chavez, Cesar, 1927– . 2. Trade-unions—Migrant agricultural laborers—United States—Officials and employees—Biography. 3. Labor leaders—United States—Biography. 4. Mexican Americans—Biography. I. Garcia, Richard A., 1941– . II. Title. III. Series.
HD6509.C48G75 1995
331.88'13'092—dc20
[B]   95–15230
                                                                CIP

César Chávez: A Triumph of Spirit is Volume 11 in *The Oklahoma Western Biographies.*

The paper in this book meets the guidelines for permanence and durability of the Committee on Production Guidelines for Book Longevity of the Council on Library Resources, Inc. ∞

6 7 8 9 10

Dedicated to the memory of César Estrada Chávez—
a man of hope, justice, and humanity

Contents

Illustrations

Unless otherwise indicated, all illustrations are from the Archives of Labor and Urban Affairs, Wayne State University.

Series Editor's Preface

IN this thoroughly researched biography Professors Richard Griswold del Castillo and Richard A. Garcia supply a particularly probing portrait of César Chávez. As the authors show, Chávez was a rather simple, straightforward person but also a man of great power, understanding, and empathy. The dilemmas of his own demanding, hardscrabble life helped him grasp similar pressures harassing millions of other agricultural workers throughout the United States.

The authors also provide illuminating glimpses of several people who surrounded Chávez, working with him, influencing his thinking, and furnishing support for his many endeavors. Chief among this central supporting cast were his wife Helen, organizer Dolores Huerta, and several other Chicano leaders. Indeed, Griswold del Castillo and Garcia are especially helpful in comparing and contrasting the leadership styles and ideologies of Chávez and other such Chicano spokesmen as Corky Gonzales, José Angel Gutiérrez, and Reies López Tijerina.

As Chávez's biographers tellingly reveal, César has become for Chicanos and many other Latinos what Martin Luther King is for African Americans—a model to whom they look for leadership and inspiration. For millions of his compatriots, Chávez also embodies a classic American story, that of the newcomer struggling to participate in the nation's society and economy on more equal terms than many of its citizens wish to grant. Scholars and general readers alike will appreciate the warmth and understanding with which the authors treat these facets of their subject.

Most of all, the authors present the engrossing story of a courageous man whose life and ideas have influenced the lives of multitudes of Americans. Through his inspired, forceful, and committed leadership, César Chávez deservedly has become a hero for millions of others. By delineating the influence of a notable person on the history of the United States, Professors Griswold del Castillo and Garcia have achieved the major goal of the Oklahoma Western Biographies series.

RICHARD W. ETULAIN

University of New Mexico

Preface

CÉSAR Chávez's death in April 1993 shocked some, surprised many, and passed unnoticed by others. Newspapers throughout the world carried the story on the front page. Chávez was a person who in death, as in life, was considered to be the embodiment of many themes, many causes, many personas. To some he was a union leader, to others an American reformer, and to still others he was an American Gandhi. To many Mexican Americans and young Chicanos he was a spiritual leader. In the 1990s, César Chávez's death has revived an interest in his life, his historical importance, and his legacy.

Regardless of what perspective is taken on Chávez, he was of considerable political and ethnic importance. U.S. President Clinton, Pope John Paul, President Salinas de Gortari of Mexico, and others sent telegrams of condolences to the funeral at Delano, California. President Clinton urged all Americans to "reflect on and honor the life of this distinguished leader, veteran, and American." Mexican President Salinas praised Chávez for his work for all Mexican workers and held him as an example of a courageous leader. Pope John Paul focused on Chávez's spirituality, courage, and untiring efforts for the workers, the poor, and the marginal. Comedian Paul Rodriguez, the son of a farm worker, stated the obvious most clearly: "Chávez was the closest thing we've [Mexican Americans and Latinos] had to a national hero"; and Dolores Huerta, cofounder with Chávez of the United Farm Workers union in 1965, said, "César believed in the philosophy of St. Francis of Assisi: you can't really feel the pain of the poor unless you are one of them." The importance of Chávez's life was framed by the seemingly innocent question asked by one of the funeral marchers, Al Escobedo, of Oxnard, California: "Can't we have a national holiday honoring César Chávez?"

César Chávez, like John F. Kennedy, Robert Kennedy, Martin Luther King Jr., Malcolm X, and other heroes of the 1960s, lived and died shrouded in a veil of truths, lies, perceptions, and myths. Each of their lives was intertwined with some of the major historical, cultural, and societal changes and crises of the last part of the twentieth century. Each of them embodied turning points in the lives of many individuals and in the communal perspectives and sociopolitical opinions of their times. They were spiritual and moral gauges of the era.

Our text, written in a narrative and interpretive style, examines Chávez's life: his courageous acts, his turning points, and the many perceptions about his persona. Throughout this book we will examine a man who came to believe that there was a basic, reciprocal relationship between God, man/woman, truth, justice, and nature. Chávez believed that everyone, regardless of class, race, religion, or generation, could understand and accept this if they were to examine the "facts" he presented: facts that showed oppression and injustices. Ultimately, he was a man who lived a simple life and preached a simple guiding dictum: *Sí Se Puede* (Yes, it can be done). Faith in humanity, a belief in action, and a need for courage, as well as an unadulterated belief in God, shaped his personal, intellectual, and spiritual self.

We believe that Chávez's life has a meaning that extends beyond those of labor or even ethnic history. More than a well-known labor and union leader of the farm workers, more than a spiritual leader of the Chicano movement, he was an American reformer. As an organizer versed in the Saul Alinsky method of community empowerment, he never varied from this philosophy of human rights, although others shaped and defined his ideological and political direction. With a close cadre of advisors, including his alter ego, Dolores Huerta, he breathed life into the union. Chicano student radicals as well as the Mexican-American middle class considered him to be a spiritual and political leader.

Chávez's life can be seen as a biographical prism through which to examine the major events and issues that have affected Mexican Americans in the United States—especially with regard to the centrality of sacrifice and struggle in Mexican-American culture and thought. Through Chávez we are able to better understand contemporary Chicano history. Above all, Chávez, as seen here, is the means by which we can comprehend the crossroads of culture, ethnicity, and justice in the United States.

His life spans a crucial period of contemporary culture and twentieth-century Western experience. This period saw the emergence of Mexican Americans from demographic and political obscurity. Some have moved to national prominence and importance. The economic importance of Mexican Americans in the development of the American West, especially in the twentieth century, has been notable. Overall, Chávez's life mirrors major themes in Mexican-American history: Mexican immigration during the 1920s; forced repatriation of the 1930s; segregation of Mexicans in public schools; the contributions of Mexican Americans during World War II; the Zoot Suit riots in Los Angeles; the formation of Mexican-American organizations that fought to advance Mexican-American civil and political rights; the Chicano movement of the 1960s and early 1970s; the emergence of a conservative political backlash in the 1980s; and the importance of "new immigration" in the 1990s. César Chávez was touched by all these historical events and his story is that of not only an individual but a collective experience. In short, this biography—the study of one man's interaction with the historical forces of his era—tells how he was influenced by history along with how he worked to change it.

Ultimately, César Chávez's significance is largely moral. In an age when we are increasingly aware of the lack of moral values within U.S. society, Chávez stands out as one of the bright lights in the nation's development—proof that America still has men and women of rare courage and conviction who base their lives on a righteous cause. César's life was one built on fundamental moral principles. To a large extent these principles have also been part of the Mexican-American heritage: self-sacrifice for others, courageous struggle despite overwhelming odds, respect for races and religions, nonviolence, belief in a divine soul and moral order, a rejection of materialism, and a faith in the moral superiority of the poor, as well as a central belief in justice. These values César Chávez championed. They are also values that have been part of the Mexican culture for more than five centuries. But Chávez represented the struggles of all peoples in America to achieve a better life. He represented a moral code that might point a way out of the dilemmas America confronts as it enters the twenty-first century.

Many individuals and institutions have contributed to the writing of this book. San Diego State University made several grants that enabled travel and research time. Kaiser Foundation provided a generous grant for archival research at the United Farm Workers (UFW) collection at Wayne State University in Detroit, Michigan. The Committee on International Education granted a five-month research and teaching fellowship in Mexico that facilitated much of the writing and rewriting. California State University at Hayward contributed course reduction time that also expedited our work. Special thanks go to Jacques E. Levy for permission to quote from his work, *César Chávez: Autobiography of La Causa*, and to Richard Etulain, series editor of the University of Oklahoma Western Biographies, for his thorough and detailed reading of the early drafts; also to Maryann Griswold del Castillo for her detailed critique of the manuscript.

Finally, in listing those who helped us, we must mention César Chávez himself. He generously gave us union publications and other documents as well as several hours of interview time. These conversations enabled us to interpret sources and get a better sense of Chávez's personal views on crucial issues. César, along with other union officials, past and present, helped us better understand the farm workers' struggle.

RICHARD GRISWOLD DEL CASTILLO

RICHARD A. GARCIA

César Chávez

CHAPTER I

Early Years

God writes in exceedingly crooked lines.
CÉSAR CHÁVEZ

DUST hung heavy on the horizon, blending in the distance with the blue-green combination of earth and growing plants. The smell of burned weeds mingled with that of fresh, wet earth. A family of farm workers, each of them bending in the early morning sun, swayed rhythmically to a silent beat, moving slowly, almost imperceptibly down endless furrows. The crop, lettuce, called for close work with a short-handled hoe: thinning—chopping out ten, fifteen, twenty seedlings, allowing one to remain and survive, to grow to maturity.

The Chávez family worked together in silence. The smallest member was a thirteen-year-old boy with large black eyes and jet black hair. For a week, he and his parents and older brother had worked in this field: waking at three in the morning to meet the labor contractor who would drive them to the field in a rattling bus. Then, the day done at about four in the afternoon, they would take the same dusty road back to Calexico. Together they hoped to earn twenty dollars that week, after paying for the bus ride, for a one-room shack in the labor camp, and for miscellaneous expenses. The balance would barely be enough for gas to travel the one hundred miles to the next agricultural valley, where they hoped to find work the next week.

This precarious existence of grueling toil and bare subsistence was the life of Librado Chávez and his family for ten years, after they had been ordered off their family farm in

Arizona. They were now migrant workers, people without a home, a future, or a promise. Formed by this depressing condition, the boy César Chávez matured into a young man. The years of migration and hunger, without a fixed home, following the crops throughout California, burned deep impressions in his young mind. As an adult, Chávez would labor to assure that other families would not have to endure similar experiences.

The story of César Chávez's early development as a boy and young man provides insights into the career he was to have as an internationally known labor leader. He was formed by his family and their moral teachings, the legacy of his Mexican past, and the discrimination and deprivation he and his family endured as migrant farm workers.

The first members of César Chávez's family moved to the United States in the 1880s when César's grandfather and namesake, Cesario, with his wife and children, fled the grinding poverty and injustices of the hacienda system. They crossed into the United States at El Paso, Texas, and traveled to Arizona, where they established a freight business and homesteaded a quarter section of land in the North Gila Valley. César's father, Librado, was two when they crossed the Rio Grande frontier. In Arizona, Librado worked with his father on the farm until he was thirty-eight, when he married Juana Estrada. In time, Librado became a small businessman, running a grocery store, an auto repair shop, and a poolroom about twenty miles north of Yuma, Arizona. César Estrada Chávez was born there on 31 March 1927.

The early years of the depression did not drastically affect the Chávez family. They were saved from unemployment by a large extended family that provided a built-in clientele for their business. The Mexican community, composed mostly of small landholders and farmers, was almost self-sufficient, not dependent on industrial employment or relief. In the midst of the depression, perhaps to increase the family's security, César's father decided to expand his business to include a forty-acre parcel surrounding the store and to purchase the land he took out a loan from a supposedly friendly lawyer. Within a few years he was unable to make the payments. An Anglo property owner working with the lawyer pressured Librado so that he was forced to sell his store to make a partial payment on back taxes. Also contributing to the family's economic problems was Librado's granting of credit to the hundreds of friends and relatives who likewise were experiencing hard times. Librado did not have the cash to meet his financial obligations. After the loss of their business, the Chávez family moved in with César's grandmother, Mama Tella. His grandfather, Cesario, had died several years earlier. About a mile from their old store, Mama Tella owned an old adobe house and a 160-acre homestead, half of which was planted in cash crops, the remainder providing pasture for cows and horses. The family was barely self-sufficient.

Chávez remembered life on his grandmother's farm as a secure and happy time. He was surrounded by people who influenced his formation as a young man. Chávez's mother, for example, shaped his views about nonviolence and morality. She spent a great deal of time with her four children (who now included Librado, "Lenny," who was born soon after they moved in with Mama Tella). She told them many *cuentos* (stories) and gave them *consejos* and *dichos* (advice and sayings), all with a moral point. Chávez later remembered: "I didn't realize the wisdom in her words, but it has been proven to me so many times since." Because his mother's patron saint was St. Eduvigis, a Polish duchess who gave her wealth to the poor, she, Chávez remembered, "had made a pledge never to turn away anyone who came for food, and there were a lot of ordinary people who would come and a lot of hobos, at any time of the day or night. Most of them were white [non-Mexican]."

Another important moral influence on young Chávez was his grandmother's religious teaching. Although nearly one hundred years old in 1937, Mama Tella taught the Chávez children their catechism and church history in preparation for their first communion. She instilled a love of the rituals of the Roman Catholic Church, the Sunday masses, Christmas and Easter obligations, and special feast days. All his life, César would rely on the spiritual strength he gained from attending mass.

While living with Mama Tella on the 160 acres, César and the oldest children had experienced their first discrimination in school. Like most Mexican-American families in the era before World War II, at home they spoke Spanish exclusively. César's uncle taught him how to read Spanish by holding him on his lap and reading aloud from Mexican newspapers. But at the public school, Anglo-American students made fun of the Chávez children's accents and teachers punished them for speaking in Spanish. Chávez's school experiences typified those of hundreds of thousands of Mexican Americans in that era. "When we spoke Spanish, the teacher swooped down on us. I remember the ruler whistling through the air as its edge came down sharply across my knuckles." If corporal punishment was bad, embarrassment and public humiliation for mispronounced words were worse. Thus, in his early school years in Yuma, Chávez first encountered racism. Anglo children contemptuously called him a "dirty Mexican"; and when fights erupted between Anglos and Mexicans on the playground, the principal always sided with the Anglo kids. On one occasion, when the teacher heard César describe himself as a Mexican, she insisted that he not use that word. She insisted that he was an American, not a Mexican. Confused, he asked his mother what all this meant. She explained that because he had been born in the United States he was an American citizen, "but I didn't known what 'citizen' meant. It was too complicated."

Another influence on César at the Yuma homestead was the political legacy of the Mexican Revolution he learned through family stories and legends. During the summers, the children would sleep outside under mosquito netting and overhear the conversations of the adults—"about the haciendas, how the big landowners treated the people, about the injustices, the cruelties, the exploitation." In addition, Chávez heard about the political corruption his grandfather witnessed in El Paso and about the political activities of his father and relatives as they organized a power bloc in the Gila Valley in the 1930s. Over time, Chávez's father became influential within the Mexican community by assisting at fund-raisers for candidates and encouraging Mexican-American voters to vote as a group for the candidates he supported.

Local political events soon changed the Chávez family drastically, forcing them to join the stream of rural migrants flowing west to California. César's father still owed $4,080 in back taxes and interest on his homestead. Convinced that only a direct appeal to the governor could save them, Librado traveled to Phoenix to petition the governor, but to no avail. A local banker who owned adjacent land refused to grant a loan, even though Librado qualified for it under federal guidelines. On 29 August 1937, the state took legal possession of their land, although they were allowed to remain there for another year.

Meanwhile Librado and other relatives had left Yuma to look for work in California. When they found good temporary jobs, they sent for their families. But after working several seasons away from home in California the Chávez clan was still unable to raise the money to buy back the farm and they had to sell it to the banker-grower for $1,750. Chávez remembered when the deputy sheriff came to the adobe: "He had papers that told us we had to leave or go to jail. My mother came out of the house crying. We children [César was turning ten at the time] knew there was trouble, but we were confused, worried. For two or three days the deputy came back, every day . . . and [then] we had to leave. When we left the farm, our whole life was upset, turned upside down. We had been part of a very stable community, and we were about to become migrant workers. We had been uprooted."

In 1939, when the Chávez family left Arizona, more than 250,000 migrants lived in California, remnants of the dust bowl and farm failures of the 1930s. These were families whose tragic lives were captured by John Steinbeck in his novel *The Grapes of Wrath* and by Dorothea Lange in her moving photographs. Throughout the depression, a growing army followed the crops. From the irrigated desert of the Imperial Valley, through California's lush Central Valley, they harvested all kinds of fruits and vegetables, working their way up to the apple and peach orchards of Oregon and Washington. They were a multinational people: poor whites, Okies and Arkies from the Midwest, black sharecroppers from the deep South, Mexican immigrants and Mexican-American migrants from Southwestern states, dispossessed urban workers of every nationality. Despite their differences in language and background, they shared a daily struggle against insecurity, hunger, and fear.

A HISTORY OF EXPLOITATION

The Mexican, Mexican-American, and black migrant agricultural workers confronted an additional obstacle: racism—ethnic discrimination. Farming and ranching in California depended on the exploitation of racial groups. Historically, during the Spanish and Mexican period the missions and ranchos had depended on native peoples to do the farming. In the nineteenth century, Anglo-American farmers had preferred Chinese workers, but when these laborers began to organize to demand better treatment, the farmers recruited workers from Japan and India. Each new ethnic and racial group was seen as undesirable for farm labor when it began organizing in ways that threatened to raise wages.

During the 1920s, California growers realized the value of recruiting hundreds of thousands of displaced Mexican immigrants to work in the fields. In the Midwest, industrialists also recruited thousands of Mexican immigrants to drive down wages and work as strikebreakers in the steel mills in Gary, Indiana, and in the stockyards and packinghouses of south

Chicago. As a result, a Mexican barrio of almost a million would develop in Chicago by 1980. Also during the 1920s, farmers in Colorado, Wyoming, Utah, Iowa, and Nebraska began importing temporary Mexican migrant laborers; and in the Southwest, growers began recruiting Mexicans anxious to leave their country. The Mexican Revolution corresponded in time with the rapid development of new agricultural lands in California and south Texas. The violence of the civil war in Mexico created an uprooted and willing labor force that could easily be rounded up by labor contractors (*enganchadores*) and sent north and west to work in the fields and factories. During periods of economic depression, first in 1921 and again in 1929, Mexican workers were expelled from the country, to make room for workers born in the United States, thereby reducing the economic and political costs of unemployment.

Again in the 1930s, Mexican immigrants had to vie with others for seasonal work. Nativeborn United States citizens competed with the Mexican-born, or those of Mexican origin. Hardly anyone subscribed to the distinction made by Chávez's grade-school teacher. Mexicans, whether or not U.S. citizens, were considered to be foreign workers, not entitled to the same rights as "American" workers. Thus racism played an important role in American business, dividing workers and keeping wages down. Generally, farmers preferred Mexican workers over others because of their reputed docility. The Mexicans' eagerness to work supposedly made them better able to withstand the fierce heat and backbreaking monotony of field work. The growers considered Mexicans a slavelike labor force. One grower expressed a common attitude toward a Mexican laborer in this period: "He is a fellow easy to handle and very quiet in his living, a man who lends himself very well to ranch labor, a man who gives us no trouble at all. He takes his orders and follows them." Another grower expressed the class distinctions between the growers and their laborers: "We protect our farmers here in Kern County. They are our best people. They are always with us. They keep the country going. . . . But the Mexicans are trash. They have no standard of living. We herd them like pigs."

In Arizona, however, rural isolation insulated the Chávez family from the virulent racism that characterized relations between Anglos and Mexicans in the factorylike farms of California. As long as Chávez family members stayed within their isolated rural community, they did not have to worry about being deported or repatriated by the border patrol. Once they joined the migrant stream, this move became a real possibility.

On the first night of their journey to California in the old family car, they were stopped by a border patrol officer on suspicion of of being undocumented Mexican immigrants. Although César's mother had lived in the United States since the age of five months, she did not speak English, and neither did César's brother and sister. After five hours of grueling interrogation in the middle of the desert, the border patrol let the family go.

Others were not so fortunate. During the 1930s, about 500,000 Mexicans were repatriated or deported back to Mexico. "Repatriation" was a polite term for what happened: the majority of Mexican immigrants, whether in the United States legally or not, were cajoled, frightened, intimidated, and tricked by federal and local officials into returning to Mexico. This was an attempt to lower the numbers of people on relief and to provide more employment for United States citizens by "getting rid of the Mexican." Many who left were U.S.–born but had parents who (like the Chávezes) were long-term residents without papers. The most energetic repatriation campaigns took place in Texas and southern California, where the largest Mexican populations lived. During the early 1930s, about 132,000 Mexicans were forced to leave Texas; another 100,000 were shipped by train, bus, and truck from Los Angeles to points south of the border. Many labor unions and nativist political associations, such as the Immigration Restriction League, supported repatriation as well as other immigration-restriction measures. The Mexican government, through its consulate offices in the Southwest, encouraged repatriation, hoping to attract skilled workers and thereby bolster national pride. The Mexican government attempted to settle *repatriados* on marginal lands in colonies, but these efforts were largely a failure. The repatriation campaign reached its height during a period of intense anti-Mexican sentiment in 1931–1932. Voluntary repatriation, stimulated by fears and by the lack of jobs and relief funds, continued throughout the 1930s.

TEENAGER MIGRANT

For the next ten years the Chávez family worked as farm laborers, moving from farm to farm up and down California and taking other odd jobs to supplement their income when there was no farm work. During this period, as a teenager, César encountered conditions he would dedicate the rest of his life to changing: wretched migrant camps, corrupt labor contractors, meager wages for backbreaking work, bitter racism.

Working the vegetable and fruit harvest in Brawley, next the fields in Oxnard, and later up the San Joaquin Valley in the fall following the cotton crop, the Chávez family was one of 25,000 to 30,000 migrant families who were always on the move, frequently hungry, just barely able to earn enough money to buy gas to get to the next farm. In Oxnard, the Chávez family had to spend one winter living in a tent that was soggy from rain and fog. They used a 50-gallon can for a stove and tried to keep wood for fuel dry inside the tent. The children did odd jobs around town; the adults tried to find work. Moving north to the San Joaquin Valley, they stayed in labor camps, living in tiny tarpaper-and-wood cabins without indoor plumbing and with a single electric light. There were no paved streets and in the winter the ground turned into a quagmire.

These conditions were made worse by exploitive labor contractors who frequently owned or managed the camps. The contractor would deduct the workers' rent from their pay, at exorbitant rates, and usually operated a company store that charged sky-high prices for basic food and supplies. César's memory of the labor contractors' exploitation of his family was vivid: "On payday we even had to argue with them for our pay. If payday was supposed to be Saturday, some of them didn't pay until Monday. We'd probably find him drunk in a bar, and he'd say, 'Well, the boss didn't give me a check,' even though we knew the grower had already paid him."

The evils of the contractor system were multiple, and the Chávez family encountered them all. Contractors would over-recruit workers and then lower the announced wage. They would short-weight or short-count the sacks or boxes of produce and pocket the difference. They would make deductions for Social Security and not report them. Occasionally workers would have to buy their jobs; other contractors would demand sexual favors from female workers. When, in 1942, César's father was involved in a car accident and could not work for a month, César quit school (he had completed the eighth grade) and worked full-time in the fields to help support his family. He did not want his mother to have to continue to work. César and his older brother and sister were supporting a family that now included Lenny and Vickie. Together, Richard, Rita, and César thinned lettuce and sugar beets; in winter they planted onions. They often worked with the short-handled hoe, a backbreaking instrument. César recalled the crucifying job of thinning: "I would chop out a space with the short-handle hoe in the right hand while I felt with my left to pull out all but one plant as I made the next chop. There was a rhythm, it went very fast. . . . It's like being nailed to a cross. You have to walk twisted, as you're stooped over, facing the row, and walking perpendicular to it. You are always trying to find the best position because you can't walk completely sideways, it's too difficult, and if you turn the other way, you can't thin." Later, as a union leader, Chávez would lead the attack to outlaw the short-handled hoe, remembering it from his personal experience and because it caused permanent back-injury to thousands of farm workers.

The ethnic prejudice that César encountered during this

migrant period also shaped his life. Chávez remembered, "I still feel the prejudice, whenever I go through a door. I expect to be rejected, even when I know there is no prejudice there." Many incidents sharpened César's awareness of anti-Mexican racism. When he was age eleven and living in Brawley, the police would not let Mexican (or Mexican-American) shoeshine boys into the Anglo neighborhoods. On one occasion, he and his brother crossed over to a diner without their shoeshine box. He saw a sign, WHITE TRADE ONLY, in the window but went in anyway. When they ordered a hamburger, the countergirl told them with a laugh, "We don't sell to Mexicans." Chávez left in tears, the memory of that laugh ringing in his ears "for twenty years—it seemed to cut us out of the human race." On other occasions, in the San Joaquin Valley, the Chávez family was rejected by other Anglo merchants. In 1944, in Delano, where the family had established a winter base, César challenged the segregated theater system by refusing to sit in the Mexican section. The manager called the police, who took him to the police station and held him for about an hour.

Discrimination extended to school classrooms. Like thousands of other migrants, Chávez attended scores of schools because his family had to be constantly on the move. Many of these schools were still segregated, following a practice that had taken root in California in the 1920s. The worst part was being treated as a nonperson by the teachers and administrators in these schools. Chávez recalled: "Their indifference was incredible. When you went into school for the first time, the principal and a teacher would discuss where they should put you, right in front of you. They would make you run laps around the track if they caught you speaking Spanish, or a teacher in a classroom would make you write 'I won't speak Spanish' on the board 300 times, or I remember once a teacher hung a sign on me that said 'I am a clown, I speak Spanish.'"

Unfortunately, these and similar ordeals were part of the everyday life of Mexican farm workers and their children in the Southwest in the 1930s and 1940s. From these experiences César learned that segregation was an evil, making people feel excluded and inferior. As a result, one of the main tenets of his later organizing philosophy was that neither racial nor ethnic prejudice had a place within a farm workers' union movement. Because of his experiences as a boy growing up in rural California, he would find common ground with the civil rights activists of the 1950s and 1960s.

FIRST TASTE OF UNION WORK

Chávez's migrant period also introduced him to the practical difficulties of organizing a union of farm laborers. While moving from crop to crop, his father joined several unions—the Tobacco Workers, the Cannery Workers, the National Farm Labor Union (NFLU), and the Packing House Workers. The family also participated in many strikes during the late 1930s and 1940s. By being part of these activities, the Chávez family became part of a long tradition of organized struggle in the fields, a tradition dating from the turn of the century.

One of the earliest agricultural unions, organized by Mexicans in California, was the Imperial Valley Workers' Union (La Unión de Trabajadores del Valle Imperial). In 1928, with more than 2,700 members, the union went on strike. They wanted an increase in the piecework rate for cantaloupe picking, a reform in the labor contractor system, and drinking water, outhouses, and accident insurance for workers. The growers tried to end the strike by getting court orders against picketing, organizing armed vigilante groups, getting the police to make mass arrests, and by Red-baiting the union leadership with hysterical media accounts. Within a year the growers defeated the union. In the process they established a pattern for handling future farm-labor strikes that would last well into the 1970s.

Despite this early setback, California became a focus for labor organizing activity in the 1930s. In 1933, for instance, 5,000 Mexican berry pickers in El Monte organized a union,

the Confederación de Uniones de Campesinos y Obreros Mexicanos (CUCOM), which went on strike to raise hourly pay.
Strikers were joined by a more militant, Communist-led labor
union that included some Mexican organizers, the Cannery
and Agricultural Workers' Industrial Union (C&AWIU), with
7,000 workers. Because the growers were Japanese farmers
who feared a nativist backlash, the Mexican union won its
wage demands.

The C&AWIU moved on to organize cotton workers in the
San Joaquin Valley. The result was a prolonged and violent
cotton strike in 1933, in which 12,000 cotton pickers, 75 percent of whom were Mexican, confronted the powerful San
Joaquin Valley Agricultural Labor Bureau, representing the
cotton growers. Because of the labor surplus generated by the
depression, the growers had lowered piecework wages to star-
vation level: 15 cents per hour. Thereafter, events followed the
pattern established in 1928 in the cantaloupe strike: evictions,
court orders, arrests, and violence. The growers hired goons
and strikebreakers who surrounded union meetings at the
towns of Pixley and Arvin and killed three farm workers.
During the strike, hospitals refused to admit wounded and
sick striking farm workers and their families. People starved.
No relief or charity funds were available and eventually nine
infants died of malnutrition. When the violence and suffering
could no longer be ignored, state and federal officials intervened to negotiate a compromise settlement. The strike ended.

Throughout the 1930s, hundreds of agricultural strikes occurred. Many were spontaneous walkouts in protest over the
numerous injustices. Of one such strike, Chávez said: "Once
in Wasco we were picking cotton when another farm worker
started arguing he was being shortchanged in weight. We argued for the worker, and when he quit, we quit too. We quit
many jobs over such arguments. . . . We weren't afraid to
strike, but those strikes weren't on the picket line. We would
leave and try to take as many people as we could and go work
elsewhere."

In the 1940s, the Chávez family joined the National Farm Labor Union (NFLU), which had been organized under the American Federation of Labor (AFL) as a branch of the Southern Tenant Farmers Union. Led by Hank Hasiwar and Ernesto Galarza, the union launched a number of strikes throughout California. Along with several thousand Mexican workers, the Chávez family participated in a cotton strike organized by the union in 1948. A few months earlier, the union had begun a strike against the Di Giorgio Corporation, a family-run corporation and one of the largest fruit growers in the United States. The struggle against the Di Giorgios lasted two and a half years. It was broken by the use of a government injunction under the Taft-Hartley Act, the recruitment of *braceros* (contract laborers) as strikebreakers, and Red-baiting by the California Senate Committee on Un-American Activities.

Ernesto Galarza—mentioned above as one of the NFLU organizers—was a Mexican-American author, sociologist, and labor expert with a doctorate (Ph.D.) from Columbia University. As a predecessor of César Chávez in organizing farm workers in California, he foreshadowed César's activity: he organized a consumer boycott against Di Giorgio table grapes. Galarza pioneered the idea of organizing picket lines outside supermarkets, encouraging mass support for the NFLU farm workers. Favoring the NFLU boycott, students and clergy from the San Francisco Bay Area lent their support to the grape strike and boycott. As the union's director of research and education, Galarza helped produce a movie, *Poverty in the Valley of Plenty,* criticizing the conditions farm workers faced in working on the Di Giorgio farm. The Di Giorgios sued for libel and won, and the film was destroyed. Later, Galarza worked with the AFL-CIO in organizing farm workers through the Agricultural Workers Organizing Committee (AWOC) and acted as an adviser to César during his early years of leadership in a similar, larger strike and boycott.

During the 1940s, when Galarza was beginning his organizing efforts, César was still a young man. Like many teenagers of his generation, he had briefly participated in the cultural phenomenon known as the pachucos. In this era, young Mexican Americans in California were usually called either Mexicans or pachucos, depending on the circumstance. The term *Chicano* was used almost exclusively by barrio residents to refer to recently arrived Mexican immigrants. In 1944, aged seventeen, César had flirted briefly with the pachuco lifestyle. This distinctive subculture flourished among younger Mexican Americans in rebellion against their parents' conventional values. The pachucos adopted their own music, language, and dress. The style was to wear a zoot suit, a flamboyant long coat, with baggy, pegged pants, a porkpie hat, a long keychain, and shoes with thick soles. They called themselves pachucos, a word of uncertain origin generally referring to U.S.-born Mexican youth who dressed in a distinctive style and spoke *calo*, a highly inventive slang-Spanish. Chávez said of his pachuco days: "We needed a lot of guts to wear those pants, and we had to be rebellious to do it, because the police and a few of the older people would harass us. But it was the style, and I wasn't going to be a square."

Like most zoot-suiters, Chávez had run-ins with the police, who usually considered pachucos potential gang members and criminals. In the 1940s, especially in southern California, hysteria had been mounting over pachuco gangs, including periodic mass arrests accompanied by sensational publicity in the *Los Angeles Times*. In the summer of 1942, the Sleepy Lagoon case made national news, when nine teenage members of the 38th Street gang were put on trial for the murder of José Díaz in an abandoned quarry pit. The case generated an outburst of anti-Mexican sentiment, because all Mexican-American youths were characterized in the press as "baby gangsters" and pachuco hoodlums. The nine young men were convicted and sentenced to long prison terms at San Quentin, but in 1944 the Sleepy Lagoon Defense Committee, a group of liberal civil rights activists, including Carey McWilliams, managed to reverse the conviction.

Soon after the Sleepy Lagoon case, a series of Zoot Suit riots erupted in Los Angeles, San Jose, Oakland, Delano, San Diego, and elsewhere. In reality these so-called riots were a series of attacks, by servicemen and police, on zoot suit-wearing Mexicans. The most serious incident took place in Los Angeles. For more than a week following 6 June 1943, hundreds of servicemen went on a rampage through East Los Angeles and the downtown district. Carey McWilliams, a lawyer and eyewitness, described the scene in his book, *North from Mexico:*

> Marching through the streets of downtown Los Angeles, a mob of several thousand soldiers, sailors, and civilians, proceeded to beat up every zoot-suiter they could find. Pushing its way into the important motion picture theaters, the mob ordered the management to turn on the house lights and then ranged up and down the aisles dragging Mexicans out of their seats. Street cars were halted while Mexicans, and some Filipinos and Negroes, were jerked out of their seats, pushed into the streets and beaten with a sadistic frenzy.

After strong protests by the Mexican government, Los Angeles was declared off-limits to the military and the city government passed an ordinance making the wearing of the zoot suit a misdemeanor.

César was working in the fields with his family in the San Joaquin Valley when the Zoot Suit riots erupted in Los Angeles. During the off-season, the Chávez family lived in the San Jose barrio of Sal Si Puedes (literally, *get out if you can,* a phrase capturing the ironic humor of its seasonal residents). During the war, about the only way a Mexican youth could escape the barrio and the grinding toil of the fields was to join the armed services. Hundreds of thousands of Mexican-American young men joined the military, motivated by patriotism, machismo, or poverty. In 1944, when he was seventeen, César joined the U.S. Navy and like thousands of other Mexican Americans discovered another world. Arriving in San Diego for boot camp, he found that Mexicans were not the only persons discriminated against because of their nationality or language. Chávez remembered: "I saw this white kid fighting, because someone had called him a Polack and I found out he was Polish and hated that word Polack. He fought every time he heard it. I began to learn something, that others suffered too."

After César's training, the navy sent him to the South Pacific, where he served as a coxswain apprentice in Saipan, assisting in ferrying ships' pilots in and out of the harbor. Later he was transferred to Guam, where he worked as a painter. When César got out of the navy in 1946, he returned to his family in Delano and resumed work in the fields. The next year he got involved with the NFLU's cotton strike in the San Joaquin Valley: his father had become a member of Galarza's union. His family joined a car-caravan of strikers and participated in huge open-field meetings. There, César learned firsthand about strike issues. As he later recalled: "Some very good stuff was developed at these meetings, but I wanted to do more than just be there. I wanted to help. I didn't know anything about unions." Still, Chávez volunteered to sweep out the union headquarters and did small jobs around the migrant camps. After two weeks, through mediation of the state's agricultural labor bureau, the strike ended with a victory for the workers.

YOUNG FAMILY MAN

César had been in the service for two years and had worked with his family in the fields for two years. He was twenty-one years old and ready to establish his own family. On 22 October 1948, César married Helen Fabela. They had first met at La Baratita Malt Shop in Delano when he was fifteen and the early courtship took place during harvesttime when the Chávez family was in town.

At twenty-one, César was five feet six, a slender, quiet man who seemed shy, almost inconspicuous, to those who met him. He could work long hours, conditioned by the monoto-

César, Helen, and their children, n.d. *El Macriado* photo, file 666.

nous toil in the fields. Darkened by the sun, he had black hair and soft eyes that seemed always to be alert. A year younger than César, Helen was a beautiful woman, also raised in a migrant farm-worker family. Born in Brawley in 1928 of Mexican campesino parents, she was descended from a family that had fought in the Mexican Revolution. Her family, like César's, had become migrant workers during the 1930s and 1940s. In the traditional Mexican manner, she was prepared to subordinate her own welfare to that of her family and husband. She became an important partner with César as he began to fulfill his dream of doing something to improve the lot of the farm workers.

After their wedding, César and Helen took a honeymoon visit to all the California missions. Then they returned to Delano, where he continued working in grapes and then in cotton. A few years later they moved to Crescent City in northern California, where César, his older brother Richard,

Manuel, his cousin, and other relatives got jobs with a lumber company. Helen and César lived in a little shack that Richard built for them. After a year and a half of living in overcast drizzling conditions, they were happy to move to San Jose in 1952, where César got a job in a lumber mill.

Meanwhile the César Chávez family was growing. Eight children came rapidly: Fernando in 1949, Sylvia in 1950, Linda in 1951, Eloise in 1952, Anna in 1953, Paul in 1957, Elizabeth in 1958, Anthony in 1958. Ordinarily, the financial burdens of supporting this large family would have condemned César and Helen to repeating the cycle of poverty that trapped hundreds of thousands of farmworker families, but events shaped César's life differently. He was to become a community organizer and then the leader of what would become the nation's most effective farm-labor union.

CHAPTER 2

The Education of an Organizer

A successful leader must respect himself and set an example for others. All vanities or pretensions must be done away with.

BERT CORONA

BY the late afternoon, a sticky heat in the old theater hung in the air. Underway was the organizing conference of the National Farm Workers Association. Seated at long tables, clutches of delegates dressed in open-collar work shirts and Mexican *guayaveras,* watched as the next speaker, a stocky man, strode confidently up the stairs to the microphone. He was Manuel Chávez, César's cousin, who had lived and worked with César's family since childhood. The audience fell silent and focused their attention on the huge piece of brown paper that covered the wall. With a dramatic gesture, Manuel tore it away, exposing a huge flag. On a bloodred field, a black eagle burst out of a white circle. The eagle was drawn in straight lines, a design that seemed to give it more power. Red and black in Mexico meant *huelga*—strike. In the United States, as well as in Mexico, strikes meant hunger, suffering, and violence. To the somber crowd, Manuel began to explain the meaning of the flag, and some of the audience began to nod in approval. Others got up and left the hall, angry and afraid. After speaking for a while, Manuel concluded: "When that damn eagle flies, the problems of the farm workers will be solved." Thus was born the official emblem of the National Farm Workers Association. It was a flag that would lead the California farm workers and the nation into a new era of social and political consciousness.

FATHER MCDONNELL AND FRED ROSS

César Chávez's introduction to organizing began in 1952 when he met Fr. Donald McDonnell, a Roman Catholic priest trying to build a parish in the San Jose barrio of Sal Si Puedes. McDonnell, along with Fr. Thomas McCullough, had been sent by the Archdiocese of San Francisco to work with farm laborers and Mexican bracero workers in the San Joaquin Valley. The two priests followed the migrants from camp to camp, setting up portable altars and conducting open-air confessions, ministering to the workers' spiritual needs. Quickly they learned that the migrants desperately needed something more. In San Jose, Fr. McDonnell decided to try to teach the farm workers about the church's social doctrines on labor organizing and social justice, hoping that they would begin to organize themselves to improve their lot.

César's family regularly attended mass in the barrio church and he soon became Fr. McDonnell's friend and assistant, first doing some work for the small church and then helping at mass at the bracero camps and the county jail. In the months that followed, César and Fr. McDonnell discussed the history of farm-labor organizing in California and the church's position on unions. At Fr. McDonnell's suggestion, César read the papal encyclicals on labor and books on labor history, the teachings of St. Francis of Assisi, and Louis Fisher's *Life of Gandhi*. Fisher's biography made a deep impression on Chávez, so much so that he went on to read everything that was available about India's political and spiritual leader. The Mahatma's values struck a responsive cord that echoed in Chávez's experience. Gandhi spoke about the complete sacrifice of oneself for others, about the need for self-discipline and self-abnegation in order to achieve a higher good. These were values that Mexican farm workers could understand, not only in the life of Christ but in their own family experience. Especially important to Chávez's moral development were Gandhi's ideas on nonviolence: they echoed his mother's admonitions and teachings. The philosophy of nonviolence later became a major theme in Chávez's leadership of the farm worker movement.

Another organizer at work in the Sal Si Puedes barrio was Fred Ross, sent to San Jose as an organizer for Saul Alinsky's Community Service Organization (CSO) to help Mexican Americans organize politically. During the early 1940s, Alinsky set up the Industrial Areas Foundation (IAF) in Chicago to train community leaders in poor neighborhoods to mobilize political power for social change. After World War II, the IAF targeted the Mexican communities in California and sent Ross to organize the CSO in Los Angeles. The CSO was concerned with issues that affected the urban barrios: civil rights, voter registration, community education, housing discrimination, and police brutality. In California it became organizationally independent of the Chicago organization. In Los Angeles, Ross and another organizer, Tony Ríos, succeeded in getting more than twelve thousand new voters to turn out in a 1949 election and gave victory to Edward Roybal, the first Mexican-American member of the Los Angeles City Council since 1881.

After this, Ross decided to expand the CSO base by establishing chapters throughout California. He began traveling to the major centers where Mexican Americans lived. When Ross got to San Jose, he asked Fr. McDonnell to provide him with a list of Mexican Americans who might be good leadership material. On the list was the name *César Chávez* and in June 1952 Ross one afternoon decided to visit his home. César was not at home, but Ross left word when he would return. Before Ross could knock at the door again, César went across the street to his brother Richard's house to avoid him. Months before, several Anglo social scientists had gone around the barrio asking personal questions about the way that Mexicans lived: Chávez wanted no part of this nonsense. Besides, in the barrio, a visiting Anglo usually meant trouble. Helen, however, felt that this stranger might mean a job or something positive so she pointed Ross to where César was hiding. He crossed the street and knocked on the door. Ross talked to César about arranging for a house-meeting with some of his friends so he could explain the ideas behind the CSO. Chávez agreed, but he also had a plan. "I invited some of the rougher guys I knew and bought some beer. I thought we could show this gringo a little bit of how we felt. We'd let him speak a while, and when I gave them the signal, shifting my cigarette from my right hand to the left, we'd tell him off and run him out of the house. Then we'd be even."

But during the house-meeting, Ross's sincerity impressed Chávez. Ross talked about local concerns as well as the CSO's advocacy of Mexican rights in police brutality cases. In the event, César never gave the signal and instead got rid of the rabble-rousers he had recruited. The meeting lasted two hours and César was converted. That night Fred Ross wrote in his diary: "I think I've found the guy I'm looking for." Chávez recalled: "My suspicions were erased. As time went on, Fred became sort of my hero. I saw him organize, and I wanted to learn."

THE CSO AND THE MCCARTHY ERA

For the next few months, Chávez threw himself into working as a volunteer for the CSO, helping with a voter-registration drive. Chávez's job was to go door to door to find unregistered voters and to try to convince them to fill out the forms. Soon Fred made César the chairman of the registration drive and César got his rougher friends to be registrars. Together they obtained nearly six thousand new voters in San Jose. This campaign led to a political confrontation with the city's Republican central committee, which feared a Democrat-controlled, Mexican-American political bloc. After the Republicans decided to challenge first-time Mexican-American voters at the polls, Chávez signed a letter addressed to the state attorney general protesting the Republican intimidation tactics. In return the Republicans began to accuse César of being a Communist. FBI agents were summoned to interview him and stories appeared in the local newspaper implying that he had been influenced by Communists. As a result of the controversy, a few San Jose liberals—teachers, lawyers, social workers—began to support César and challenge the innuendos. While weathering the storm, in 1953, César learned an important lesson: it is necessary to fight back to achieve progress. The experience of fighting against city officials who wanted to prevent Mexican Americans from voting gave Chávez an introduction to the art of confronting institutionalized power.

This unsavory episode in San Jose was only one of many during the McCarthy era. During this period—the early 1950s—thousands of individuals who had been organizing people to defend their civil or labor rights were accused of being Communists or Red sympathizers. On the national level, Senator Joseph McCarthy of Wisconsin hunted for Communist infiltrators in the State Department and the United States Army. In California, the Un-American Activities Committee interviewed hundreds of suspected radicals and attempted to brand them as Communists. Some had their careers ruined; others were deported.

In 1952, under pressure from anti-Communist crusaders, a new national immigration law passed Congress, reflecting the fears of the era. The Immigration and Nationality Act provided for the construction of six concentration camps to be used to intern subversives in a state of national emergency. The legislation also granted new powers to the Immigration and Naturalization Service (INS) to denaturalize United States citizens and to detain, deport, and exclude aliens. In following years, the INS deported many Mexican labor and civil rights organizers.

The early 1950s marked the height of the anti-Communist, anti-alien sentiment. In the midst of a recession, Operation Wetback took place. This systematic campaign by the INS, led by Lt. Gen. Joseph M. Swing (United States Army, Ret.), attempted to deport as many undocumented Mexicans as possible. From 1953 to 1955 almost 2 million (according the INS statistics) were either deported or forced to return to Mexico. Several court cases charged that the government had violated the civil and human rights of many immigrants and United States citizens who appeared to be Mexican. At the same time, national, middle-class Mexican-American organizations (such as the League of United Latin American Citizens and American G.I. Forum) supported the deportations. These two service groups dedicated to improving the social and economic status of Mexican Americans believed that the departure of millions of Mexican immigrants would open up more job opportunities as well as prove the patriotism of the members of their organizations. Other Mexican-American organizations, however, fought against the tide of the times. The Asociación Nacional Mexico-Americana (ANMA), for example, protested the abuses that were taking place, as did the CSO in Los Angeles, and the Los Angeles Committee for the Protection of the Foreign Born.

During the deportations, Chávez continued to work with Fred Ross and the CSO in San Jose. The CSO was primarily interested in increasing the electoral strength of Mexican Americans through voter registration and citizenship classes. César worked as an unpaid volunteer, helping Ross to organize citizenship classes in east San Jose while he continued to work full-time in the lumber yard. When César was laid off, he worked full-time as a volunteer for the CSO. His first task was to establish a service center where he could help people with their daily problems: in the process, he could establish a network of people who felt obligated to the CSO. This experience in building the service center taught César an important lesson that became the foundation of his organizing style: helping people and expecting their help in return was a way to build a strong organization. As he said later, "Once you helped people, most became very loyal. The people who helped us [in return] . . . when we wanted volunteers were the people who we had helped."

Soon Ross got permission to take Chávez on as a full-time organizer at $35 a week. He was assigned to a voter-registration drive in DeCoto (now Union City) in southern Alameda County. The drive was a success and the CSO made Chávez a statewide organizer, sending him to a series of small towns throughout the San Joaquin Valley: Hanford, Salinas, Visalia, and many others. The CSO increased his salary to $58 a week, but every two or three months he and his family had to move to a new assignment.

In the small rural town of Madera, Chávez encountered more anti-Communist paranoia. He was working with a local Pentecostal preacher to get Protestant Mexicans in Madera to join the CSO. Using songs to rally people, the preacher and César got about three hundred people to attend regular meetings. When César began training community leaders from among the volunteers, the INS examiner in Madera accused him of being a Communist. Feeling their traditional power base threatened by this newcomer, a local Roman Catholic priest and some of the town's traditional Mexican-American leaders called a secret meeting of the CSO executive board to condemn Chávez as a Communist. Chávez countered by calling a special meeting of the membership and replacing the board with farm workers, all of whom were Spanish-speaking and Protestant. The appeal to the workers for their support ended the oligarchy's power-play and gave César another political lesson in organizing: the most important supporters are the everyday workers; the middle class cannot always be trusted to support grassroots organizing.

THE BRACERO PROGRAM

In the 1950s, another issue that divided the Mexican-American community was the Bracero Program, begun by Congress in 1942. Its initial purpose was to import Mexican braceros— seasonal contract laborers—under government supervision to alleviate wartime labor shortages. Congress had repeatedly extended the program and it lasted until 1965. During the agreement and under its provisions, almost five million Mexican workers entered the United States. Legally, the braceros worked under contract; i.e., they were to be paid a specified minimum wage, receive basic amenities, and were to work only at agricultural jobs. But bracero workers complained of violations of wage agreements, substandard living quarters, exorbitant charges for food and clothing, and racist discrimination. On the other hand, growers liked the bracero program and constantly lobbied for its continuance. Growers used braceros to break strikes and to lower wages: they could dispose of these workers when they were done.

Chávez first confronted the bracero issue in 1958 when the CSO sent him to Oxnard, initially to support a local labor-union strike among the lemon workers. He found that local residents were concerned about braceros who were taking their jobs. It was their position that local residents should be given preference in hiring for agricultural jobs—and in fact Bracero Program regulations stipulated that the braceros could not be used to replace the local work force: there had to be a certified labor shortage. When Chávez began helping local residents to resolve the problem, he found a corrupt system that was controlled by the growers in league with state and federal officials. The growers falsely claimed the existence of labor shortages and then exploited the braceros by recruiting many more than were needed, giving them only occasional work at reduced pay while charging them inflated prices for room and board.

Chávez decided to attack this injustice on many fronts. First, he got CSO and community members to apply for work every day with the Farm Placement Service and compiled records of their applications and rejections. Next the CSO organized a boycott of local merchants to protest their support of the system and to pressure them to change it. Then César organized sit-down strikes in the fields to challenge the hiring of braceros. The farm workers picketed a meeting of the secretary of labor, James Mitchell, when he visited Ven-

tura for a talk; they marched with a banner depicting the
Virgin of Guadalupe to protest the lack of jobs for local residents; they pressured the Farm Placement Service office with
hundreds of complaints; and they lobbied state government
offices. The outcome of this intensive campaign was a brief
victory: state officials fired the Farm Service Placement director and some of his staff and started hiring hundreds of people
who lined up outside the CSO headquarters every day.

The experience in Oxnard was pivotal for Chávez. He experienced tactics such as the boycott, the march, the use of
religious images, and political lobbying. These tactics later
became standard techniques during the many struggles of the
United Farm Workers union.

Also in 1959, Chávez tried to organize a union to preserve
previous gains, but the CSO leadership, under pressure from
organized labor, refused to support his new venture. Chávez
realized that unless the workers negotiated formal contracts
with the growers, their victories would be short-lived. After
Chávez was reassigned to Los Angeles and appointed the national director for the CSO, factionalism destroyed his work
in Oxnard and the situation returned to what it had been
before, with braceros having preference in hiring over local
residents. Revisiting Oxnard six months later, Chávez was bitter about the loss: "I was so mad—I don't know at whom, at
the leadership and at the people for not fighting for what I
was sure was there. And I thought of all the time and energy
that I had put in. If I had the support of the CSO, I would
have built a union there. But then maybe I wasn't ready." The
Oxnard failure impressed Chávez with the importance of negotiated contracts being in place to preserve hard-won gains.
Later, in 1962, he would draw on this lesson when he set out to
organize an independent farm-workers association.

FRIENDS AND ALLIES

In 1958, others were also trying to organize farm/worker unions.
In Stockton, Fr. McCullough was building up the Agricultural

Workers Association following the failure of an NFLU tomato strike. One of the organizers there, Dolores Huerta, later became César's most trusted associate. Fred Ross, who was visiting Stockton, decided to ask the CSO chapter to help Fr. McCullough out, and he recruited Dolores—who at that time was a housewife with several small children. An attractive woman, originally from an old New Mexican family, she was completing a college degree. Outspoken, even when her views differed from those of male leaders, this dynamic, intense, fast-talking, and alert woman was assertive, aggressive: she did not fit the traditional stereotypes of a Mexican mother. In the years that followed, she became an indispensable lobbyist and political leader of the farm workers union. More will be said about Dolores Huerta in Chapter 4.

Chávez was at this time running a CSO organizing effort in De Coto. Fred introduced Dolores to him, but getting to know César took some time. Dolores said later: "I had heard a lot about him from Fred Ross—César this and César that— but I didn't really get a chance to talk to him the first time I met him, and he didn't make much of an impression on me. I forgot his face. I knew he was a great organizer, but he never showed it; it came out in the reports. He was very unassuming."

Another CSO member who met Chávez during these years was Gil Padilla, who also was to be one of the founding members of the farm-workers' union. Padilla lived in Hanford, where he did occasional farm work. He had participated in a number of agricultural strikes in the 1940s, experiencing first-hand the abuses of the labor-contracting system. He joined the CSO after hearing Chávez talk one night about the problems of farm laborers and how they should work together to improve their conditions. The next week, Padilla traveled with Chávez when he spoke in the barrio. Padilla recalled about César: "He went around talking to people about the basic problems, the real problems of the community. He was talking about how some day the people should have some sort of representation in the political structure. . . . We were thinking that if we could get someone elected, then we could get some laws that would help farm workers."

THE AWOC: AND RESIGNATION FROM THE CSO

In 1959 Fr. McCullough, Fr. McDonnell, and Dolores Huerta convinced the AFL-CIO to invest in organizing a farm workers' union. The result was the founding of the Agricultural Workers Organizing Committee (AWOC). The AFL-CIO executive committee put Norman Smith, a veteran organizer of Midwestern autoworkers, in charge and invested large sums in hiring staff. The AWOC quickly committed itself to a big lettuce strike over the bracero issue in the Imperial Valley. Because of the many problems involved in organizing migrant workers, and Smith's lack of experience in working in such a situation, the AFL-CIO became frustrated. Membership was not big enough. The AFL-CIO began to cut the funding. By 1961 Smith had been replaced by Al Green, a tough, cigar-chewing trade unionist from Stanislaus County who relied entirely on labor contractors to recruit dues-paying members. Nevertheless, the AWOC organized or assisted in organizing hundreds of strikes in the early 1960s. It kept alive the momentum of the farm worker organization, especially among the Filipino vegetable and grape workers. One of these workers, Larry Itliong, emerged as an important farm-labor organizer for the AWOC. In fact his leadership in an AWOC strike on 8 September 1965 led to an alliance with César Chávez and the beginning of the grape strike and boycott that would propel these two organizers into national prominence.

Chávez served as the state executive director of the CSO for two years. He worked with Padilla, Huerta, and others who later formed the nucleus-group of the Farm Workers Association. Among them was Antonio Orendain, a Mexican-born migrant farm worker with experience in radio and television broadcasting.

While César was working for the CSO in Los Angeles he became familiar with urban problems. Los Angeles also intro-

duced him to individuals who would become important supporters of the farm-workers' movement. One of these connections came through the CSO's work in 1960 with the Viva
Kennedy Clubs, a movement organized by the Democratic
Party to register voters among Spanish-speaking Roman Catholics in the urban barrios. Also, as CSO executive director
Chávez met and worked with the founders of the Mexican-
American Political Association (MAPA), Eduardo Quevedo
and Bert Corona, who had established a political association
in 1959 to advance the Chicano community's political interests
in the state. The CSO, MAPA, and the Viva Kennedy Clubs
became important training grounds for young Mexican Americans. At this time—the early 1960s—these youngsters were
beginning self-consciously to call themselves *Chicanos,* a slang
term Mexican Americans had used for decades to denigrate
newly arrived Mexican immigrants.

In 1962 the CSO had its annual convention in Calexico, a
border town in the Imperial Valley, way station for thousands
of migrants from Mexico. Chávez had proposed that the CSO
support a union movement for farm workers and the board
initially endorsed the project, but when the proposal came up
for a vote the convention turned it down, saying that the CSO
was not a labor organization. Following this rejection of his
project, César decided to resign his position and devote himself to building an independent farm workers' union. Before
deciding, he talked to Helen. She remembered, "[César] did
discuss it and say that it would be a lot of work and a lot of
sacrifice because we wouldn't have any income coming in.
But it didn't worry me. It didn't frighten me. . . . I never had
any doubts that he would succeed." César also talked to Dolores Huerta and Gil Padilla. They decided to continue working for the CSO, using their efforts to support farm-labor
organizing.

Soon after César's resignation, AWOC offered him a job as
a paid organizer, but he rejected the offer because he wanted
to work with "no strings attached." In the summer of 1962,

he, Helen, and their eight children traveled to Carpinteria Beach, near Santa Barbara, and took a brief camping vacation to plan their future. They had about $900 in savings and César could draw unemployment insurance for a time. They decided to use Delano as a home base for organizing their union. Richard, César's brother, lived at Delano (where he was head of the local CSO) and, if they had to, they could move in with him. Helen and César knew there was a year-round farm-labor community in Delano. It would make a solid base for a farm-worker organization.

ORGANIZING THE FWA

After the Chávez family moved to Delano in April 1962, César gassed up his battered, nine-year-old Mercury and took a three-day trip to survey the San Joaquin Valley, visiting many of the small towns where, for the next three years, he would be trying to recruit members. Helen got a job in Delano picking grapes, and César, when he returned from his trip, worked at a temporary job picking peas. They had found a cheap rental on Kensington Street and César used the garage for his headquarters. Since past failures of union efforts had made the farm workers skeptical, César decided to call his organization the Farm Workers Association, avoiding use of the term *union*. He was reading everything he could find on farm-labor unionization in the United States, and he talked to people who had been involved in past strikes. Over time, he concluded that the one fatal error, repeated over and over again, was trying to do two things at once: organize and strike. He resolved to be patient and build a strong organization before challenging the agribusiness corporations.

Using his CSO training, Chávez decided to emphasize the service-providing functions of his organization. He traveled extensively, talking to the workers to see what they thought about a union and the services it should provide. Traveling out into the fields and into the camps and *colonias* (small rural settlements) he passed out more than 80,000 questionnaires and talked to thousands of workers. In the fields, César found them reticent, so he met with them at night in house-meetings where they could be (and were) more open about their feelings. Chávez organized a modest burial-insurance program and a credit union to provide for members with financial emergencies. The funding for these projects came from the members themselves. A little later César and Helen set up a co-op to sell tires and auto supplies at cost. Helen began to work full-time for the association as the accountant and administrator of the credit union.

These organizing strategies followed traditions Mexican immigrants understood. For decades in the barrios and colonias of the Southwest, they had organized hundreds of *mutualistas*, economic and social self-help associations. In the past, these worker associations, in addition to organizing social activities, had provided death benefits and short-term loans. César encouraged farm workers to consider the Farm Workers Association (FWA) as a kind of mutualista. The union helped them with a variety of practical problems such as nonpayment of wages, late welfare checks, claims for workmen's compensation, and difficulties with the county hospital, with the schools, or with the INS. Scores of farm-worker families traveled to Delano to tell César of their troubles. His house was available to them day or night, seven days a week.

By 1962 Chávez had assembled a working team that functioned like a second family. One important addition was the Rev. Jim Drake. A Protestant minister who worked with the California Migrant Ministry (CMM), Drake was an intense young pastor with a passion to reform migrant working conditions. He and his wife Susan were soon assigned to work with Chávez by the Rev. Wayne C. Hartmire, the CMM's director. The Drakes brought with them the resources of the CMM, an ecumenical organization involved since the early 1950s in trying to help farm workers. Initially the CMM had worked with Chávez and the CSO in training activists for their rural ministry. Through his association with the CMM, Chávez gained important staff members and economic support for his fledgling association. Drake became César's stern-faced, impatient administrative assistant, traveling with him from town to town as they built the association.

César also recruited his cousin, Manuel Chávez, who was working as a car salesman in San Diego. Manuel had grown up with the Chávez family and had worked in the fields with them. César convinced Manuel to quit his job and move to Delano on a trial basis for six months. At the end of the six months, Manuel decided to stay, becoming one of César's closest associates for the next decade. César also talked Dolores Huerta into quitting her job with the CSO and moving to Delano, where she and other union volunteers were fed and housed by farmworker families.

The union grew, nourished by personal sacrifice. The Chávez family at times had to go without food and clothing to pay for union expenses. César and Manuel were reduced to asking barrio residents for food; but they found that in accepting this humble hospitality, they created a bond of trust that brought in new members. In this way they met Julio Hernandez, a farm worker from a small colonia near Corcoran, who became the first full-time staff volunteer for the union.

During these difficult times, César was offered a grant of $50,000, no strings attached, from a private foundation. He turned it down. Chávez argued that if the union accepted the grant they would have to show results, and it could take years to have tangible gains that would satisfy a foundation. Instead he wanted the workers, not a foundation, to determine when to act. He thought that the union would be stronger if, in its early years, it relied only on its membership for financial support. At this time, César was the only farm worker union official in the nation whose salary came 100 percent from the workers.

The goal was to hold an organizing convention for the union. César, his cousin Manuel, Jim Drake, Gil Padilla, Dolores Huerta, and Julio Hernandez worked through the summer of 1962, visiting house-meetings to ask farm workers to send representatives to a meeting that would formally establish the FWA. On 30 September 1962, about 150 delegates and their families went to the abandoned theater that Manuel had rented. The official name of the new organization was to be the National Farm Workers Association. The delegates voted for the union's officers, electing César Chávez president and executive officer, Dolores Huerta and Gilbert Padilla vice-presidents, and Antonio Orendain the secretary-treasurer. They voted to have dues of $3.50 a month, a considerable sacrifice for farmworkers.

In a dramatic moment during the conference, Manuel Chávez unveiled a huge copy of the union flag that he had designed. At first the colors and the symbol seemed too radical, too bold, too provocative. Chávez recalled how Manuel convinced the assembly to accept the flag: "Manuel . . . explained that the black eagle signified the dark situation in which the worker finds himself, the white circle signified hope and aspirations, and the red background indicated the toil and sacrifice that the Association and its members would have to contribute in order to gain justice for the farm workers." After some discussion, the representatives voted to accept the flag as their official emblem. They also adopted as the official motto, *Viva la Causa*. This slogan, or *grito,* eventually became widely known, echoing the aspirations of a new generation of Mexican Americans in both the fields and the urban barrios. It was a cry for justice long overdue.

The excitement of the first convention gave way to hard reality. Keeping in touch with a migratory dues-paying membership proved almost impossible and within ninety days only 12 of the original 212 members were still active. To César the effort seemed one step forward and two steps backward, but the FWA organizers persisted. As César remembered: "There were times, of course, when we didn't know whether we'd survive. We'd get members, and then they would drop out. We might go all day collecting dues and then have every single one say, 'I can't pay. I'm sorry, but I don't want to belong any more.' That happened often."

Gradually, Chávez hit on a strategy for getting new members. He would announce that a free barbecue would be held—in Corcoran, Lamont, or Delano—and hundreds of farm-worker families would show up and gladly contribute to expenses when they saw what was needed. The union would sell beer and make more than enough to cover expenses. At the barbecue they would have a booth and sign people up and give them a copy of the union's new newspaper, *El Malcriado* (The Unruly One).

During this difficult period of building membership in 1963, César was offered and refused a job as a director for the Peace Corps in Latin America. The job paid $21,000 a year and Helen's family was angry when César rejected the offer. The only source of income the Chávez family had was the $50 a week they earned from the union—not enough to live on. They still had to work periodically in the fields. But César's faith in the union was beginning to be rewarded. By 1964, the association had one thousand dues-paying members and more than fifty locals. They opened a union office in Delano at First and Albany, built with donations of labor and materials from throughout the San Joaquin Valley.

EARLY STRIKES

The next year—1965—was one of new activity for the fledgling union: national events conspired to help Chávez in his organizing efforts. In 1964, the United States and Mexico had begun negotiations to terminate the Bracero Program—the program that for years had been opposed by organized labor. Social reformers within the Democratic Party fought against the program on humanitarian grounds, and conservative Republicans regarded it as contributing to the moral decay of the United States. Because of President Johnson's astute leadership after the assassination of President John F. Kennedy in

1963, there had been a surge in congressional support for civil and labor rights. Johnson's administration succeeded in passing new civil rights legislation and in negotiating new economic incentives for Mexico to end the Bracero Program (this was the Border Industrial Program that became the basis for the construction of assembly plants or *maquiladoras* on the Mexican side of the border). Moreover, farmers were beginning to realize that their labor costs could be even cheaper if they employed undocumented Mexican workers instead of braceros. However, with the termination of the bracero program it became harder for growers to break strikes by using government agencies and these legislative changes now made it easier to organize farm workers into unions.

In March and April 1965, the FWA had its first strike when flower workers from McFarland asked Chávez to help them raise their wages. César tried to convince the workers that what they needed was a contract and to get that they would have to commit themselves to a long strike. But the most the workers were willing to do was to sign a no-work pledge. The first day of the strike, Dolores Huerta visited several workers' homes, early in the morning, to see if they were going to honor the agreement. She had to park her truck in the driveway of one house to prevent the workers from sneaking off to work. The growers, in violation of state labor codes, brought in labor contractors to try to break the strike, but the local labor commissioner refused to act. The growers gave in and agreed to a wage increase.

In the summer of 1965, migrant workers in the Porterville area went on a strike to protest an increase in rents in migrant farm-worker camps. Jim Drake and Gil Padilla led the strike, flying the flag with the black eagle and recruiting college students to help out. The organizing effort was financed by the California Migrant Ministry, despite the protests of local, grower-dominated Protestant congregations. Slowly the FWA staff was getting experience in strategies of labor organizing.

In particular, the rent strike prepared Drake and Padilla, as well as the CMM, for their involvement in the grape strike that would follow, in the fall.

Despite tremendous efforts by César and his staff, the National Farm Workers Association was barely surviving. César guessed that the union would not be ready for a sustained strike for another three or four years. He could not foresee that in September 1965 circumstances would force him and the new union to initiate what was to be the longest and most successful agricultural strike in U.S. history.

CHAPTER 3

The Birth of La Causa

The pains taken by César were never part of an act.
They were a very real extension of his philosophy that
human beings are subjects to be taken seriously.

REV. JAMES DRAKE

IN the summer of 1965, the United States was poised on the brink of a new era. Within a few years the youthful idealism that John Kennedy's brief presidency had inspired changed to a profound disillusionment with the U.S. government. It seemed that Kennedy's New Frontier could not be conquered so easily. For almost a decade, black and white civil rights advocates had been staging sit-ins, boycotts, and marches to protest second-class citizenship. Their hopes had been raised by renewed federal government commitments, and a new Civil Rights Act was due to be signed into law by the president. In Selma, Alabama, Dr. Martin Luther King led a march of 25,000 to the state capitol to protest that state's refusal to follow federal laws. In that protest, two people were killed, adding to the growing number of civil rights martyrs.

Nineteen sixty-five: it was also the year when President Johnson was working on bringing into being his vision of a Great Society, beginning with an assault on poverty. The government created the OEO (Office of Economic Opportunity) that summer, and Congress appropriated $1.3 billion for new educational programs such as Project Head Start and Upward Bound, aimed at raising the educational levels of the poor. The federal government began to pump new money into job-training programs to help the underclass. But this promise proved to be short-lived: President Johnson's growing commitment to Vietnam undercut his domestic reforms. Under the 1964 Gulf of Tonkin Resolution, Congress had given the president authority to "take all necessary measures to repel any armed attack against the forces of the United States." By June 1965, Johnson had sent more than 200,000 United States troops to Vietnam. Some Americans were opposed to the growing involvement and during the summer a coalition of students was working at organizing an antiwar march on Washington. In November, 35,000 people assembled on the mall in front of the Congress to listen to criticism of the president's policies.

This historical moment insured that César Chávez and the farm workers would become part of something called The Movement, a catchall phrase that described those individuals who shared a commitment to end the injustices of racism, the war in Vietnam, the sufferings of the poor, and the degradations of farm workers. During the 1960s Chávez and the NFWU—as the FWA later came to be known—would become one of many lightning rods for a spirit of protest that swept the land. For millions of emerging Mexican-Americans, Chávez became one of the best-known Chicano leaders, a larger-than-life symbol for struggle against exploitation and domination.

ORIGINS OF THE DELANO GRAPE STRIKE

The grape strike in Delano grew out of a protest by Filipino workers over wage inequities. Early in 1965, California growers in the Coachella Valley received a temporary dispensation from the Labor Department and had been allowed to import Mexican contract workers—braceros—to harvest the grape crop and to pay them $1.40 an hour. Meanwhile, for the same work, Filipino workers received $1.25 an hour, and Mexican Americans, $1.10. In May, fighting this wage discrimination, AWOC went on strike in the Thermal area and after ten days won a raise for both Mexican-American and Filipino workers.

Later in the summer, the grape harvest moved north into the San Joaquin Valley and growers continued to pay the old rate for nonbracero workers. On 8 September, in Delano, AWOC members led by Larry Itliong began a strike against local growers, demanding wage parity. Police began to harass the strikers and growers evicted Filipinos from their labor camps. The Filipinos appealed to Chávez and the Farm Workers Association for support and promised to respect their picket lines. Chávez issued a press release telling members not to work at the struck ranches. *El Malcriado,* the FWA newspaper, published a Spanish translation of Jack London's famous "Definition of a Strikebreaker" to shame potential scabs into not crossing the picket line. Chávez met with his staff to decide whether they should have a general meeting to vote to join the strike. They voted to have the meeting on 16 September, Mexican Independence Day.

For the next few days Chávez traveled constantly, spreading the word about the strike meeting. He prevailed on local Spanish-language disk jockeys to make announcements on their early morning shows: farm workers, irrespective of union membership, were invited to attend the strike meeting. Before the meeting, several FWA work crews had already gone on strike, leaving their jobs before a formal vote.

The evening meeting took place in Delano's Our Lady of Guadalupe church hall—a gathering of more than five hundred farm workers and their families. In an emotional revivalist atmosphere, chants of "Viva La Causa!" echoed before and after speeches in support of the strike. The hall was filled with people of all nationalities and races, blacks, Puerto Ricans, Filipinos, Arabs, and Anglos; but Mexicans and Mexican Americans predominated. Eugene Nelson, a young union volunteer, recorded Chávez's speech at this meeting and later published it in *Huelga:*

> You are here to discuss a matter which is of extreme importance to yourselves, your families and all the community. . . . A hundred and fifty-five years ago, in the state of Guanajuato in Mexico, a

padre proclaimed the struggle for liberty. He was killed, but ten years later Mexico won its independence. . . . We Mexicans here in the United States, as well as all other farm laborers, are engaged in another struggle for the freedom and dignity which poverty denies us. But it must not be a violent struggle, even if violence is used against us. . . . The strike was begun by the Filipinos, but it is not exclusively for them. Tonight we must decide if we are to join our fellow workers in this great labor struggle."

Other farm workers rose to speak and added their stories of misery and suffering to the call to join the strike. Representatives of various states in Mexico rose to pledge their support. Chávez explained the sacrifices they would have to make during a strike: the union did not have a strike fund and it would be a long struggle. Nelson recorded what happened next:

"Strike, strike!" the crowd is yelling now. "Huelga, huelga, huelga!"

"All right, we'll take a strike vote then. Everyone who is in favor of going out on strike, raise your right hand. . . ."

If there is a hand not raised, we do not see it.

"Opposed?" The question seems rather foolish by now.

"Que viva la huelga! Long live the strike!" And, "Viva!" the whole auditorium erupts in chorus, the place seems about to tumble down upon our heads.

The cheers continue for a good ten minutes, as pandemonium breaks out: "Viva Mexico! Viva Puerto Rico! Viva la causa! Viva César Chávez! Viva la union!"

The die is cast.

THE STRIKE

Soon after the strike vote, César met with Al Green, the head of AWOC, to coordinate strategy. There were rumors of an impending merger of the two unions, but this was not to take place until the next year. As a result of their discussions, a joint committee to coordinate activities was set up, and the American Workers Organizing Committee, the AFL-CIO farm workers' union, made its resources available to NFWU members. (The association, as noted in passing above, changed its name to National Farm Workers Union. This event took place in 1966.)

The Delano grape strike covered a 400 square-mile area and involved thousands of workers. The tremendous job of organizing picket lines to patrol the fields fell to inexperienced farm workers and urban volunteers, working side by side. The sheer dimensions of the ranches and farms made it impossible constantly to maintain pickets at all the entrances. Inevitably, scabs *(esquiroles)* found their way into the fields, and the union had to find ways of convincing them to join the strike. The picketed area then became a noisy place. The picketers cajoled, argued, pleaded, orated, and shamed the fieldworkers in Spanish, Tagalog, and English, trying to get them to join the strike. Picketers walked the dusty borders of the fields holding hand-painted signs, HUELGA, DELANO GRAPE STRIKER, VICTORIA!, accompanied by the FWA black eagle. Always they were observed by the police, who were ready to arrest picketers entering ranch property. Usually the ranch foreman and his staff would harass the strikers, reviling them with foul language, trying to provoke them into crossing onto farm property. Later the growers hired goons, recruited from the cities, to intimidate the strikers. Violence was a constant possibility and frequent occurrence. Ranch foremen raced their pickup trucks up and down the lines at top speed. They drove tractors between the pickets and the fields to choke the union people with dust. They sprayed them with chemicals and tried to intimidate them with shotguns and dogs. Sometimes they injured strikers. But when someone got hurt on the picket line, it often had the effect of provoking a sympathy walk-out by their own workers. The police almost never intervened to protect the picketers. They photographed the strikers and noted license-plate numbers of the picketers' cars. They arrested picketers for disturbing the peace when they shouted "Huelga!" or read Jack London's strikebreaker definition. The police were clearly in support of the growers.

Chávez saw the picket line as an educational and recruiting experience. It was the place where a person could feel the confrontation between the workers and the growers. It be-

At the grape strike at J. D. Martin Ranch, Tulare County, 1965. A shy man who embodied many causes.

came a way of building a strong membership. He would later say, "The picket line is where a man makes his commitment, and it is irrevocable; the longer he's on the picket line, the stronger the commitment. . . . The picket line is a beautiful thing, because it does something to a human being."

NONVIOLENCE

From the beginning of the strike, Chávez emphasized the importance of nonviolence as a strategy. He exhorted the volunteers and picketers: "If someone commits violence against us, it is much better—if we can—not to react against the violence but to react in such a way as to get closer to our goal.

People don't like to see a nonviolent movement subjected to violence, and there's a lot of support across the country for nonviolence. That's the key point we have going for us. We can turn the world if we can do it nonviolently."

Chávez's faith in nonviolence came from his mother's influence, his religious faith, and his self-education in reading Gandhi and other pacifists. In 1965, nonviolence also was a practical tactic for rallying national support for a labor strike. Nonviolence had become an important characteristic of the civil rights movement and it was fast becoming a tactic of the antiwar movement, although in both movements nonviolent protests would increasingly escalate into violent confrontations. For Chávez, nonviolence meant time-consuming organization and training. He used Gandhi's phrase *moral jujitsu* to describe its effect on the opposition: "Always hit the opposition off balance, but keep your principles." Chávez's commitment to nonviolence became stronger and deeper as the years passed—became more a personal article of faith, more spiritual, almost an end in itself. He told a union meeting in 1969, "There is no such thing as means and ends. Everything that we do is an end, in itself, that we can never erase. That is why we must make all our actions the kind we would like to be judged on, although they might be our last—which they might well be, who knows? That is why we will not let ourselves be provoked by our adversaries into behaving hatefully."

VOLUNTEERS

During the early days of the strike, hundreds of volunteers descended on Delano to participate. Many were clergy, responding to the message of the new liberation theology. Churchmen from the migrant ministry arrived, reporting that there was growing church support for the strike. Priests from barrio parishes traveled to the fields to offer help from the inner city. Fr. Victor Salandini volunteered to be a lobbyist in Washington, D.C. Other volunteers offered their services as legal consultants and in public relations. The Student Nonviolent Co-ordinating Committee (SNCC) and the Congress of Racial Equality sent messages of support. Later they sent volunteers. César argued with his staff about the value of the volunteers. He wanted a diversity of energies and ideas. "If we were nothing but farm workers in the Union now, just Mexican farm workers, we'd have about 30 percent of all the ideas we have. There would be no cross-fertilization, no growing. It's beautiful to work with other groups, other ideas and other customs. It's like the wood is laminated."

One of the early student volunteers to join the strike was a young Chicano from the San Francisco Bay Area named Luis Valdez. Originally from Delano, he had grown up in a migrant family but had escaped from the fields to the city and become a university student and member of the radical theater group, the San Francisco Mime Troupe. He took a creative energy to Delano that soon resulted in the organization of El Teatro Campesino (The Farm Workers Theater). Valdez had the idea of using simple, one-act skits, or *actos,* to educate farm workers about the union and the issues involved in the strike. The teatro, performed on the back of a flatbed truck in the fields, was an effective way of reaching farm workers. The actos were improvisations that dramatized, often in uproariously funny and ironic ways, the lives and struggles of field workers. The actors were themselves campesinos (farm workers): Felipe Cantu, Agustín Lira, Errol Franklin, and Gilbert Rubio were actor-founders. The teatro members followed the harvest to help with recruitment of union members. They toured the larger towns and cities to raise funds for the union, visiting university campuses and the urban barrios. In Delano, Valdez set up a Centro Campesino Cultural (Farm Worker Cultural Center) to teach migrant children about their Mexican heritage through art, music, dance, and *teatro.* He explained the need for this effort: "This is a society largely hostile to our cultural values. There is no poetry about the United States. No depth, no faith, no allowance for human contrariness. No soul, no mariachi, no chili sauce, no pulque, no mysticism, no *chingaderas* (fooling around)." Luis stayed with the NFWU for several years and then moved his group to San Juan Bautista. Later he broke into Hollywood with his stage production, *Zoot Suit,* and the movie, *La Bamba.*

THE STRIKE BECOMES NATIONAL

César's main activity during the early months of the strike was to travel around the state to the college campuses to give speeches and galvanize support for the striking workers. In October, he and Wendy Gospel drove from Delano to the Bay Area where he spoke at U.C. Berkeley, San Francisco State, Mills College in Oakland, and Stanford University. They raised more than $6,500 in donations and got students to flood the Delano chief of police with phone calls and letters protesting the arrest of strikers. Chávez's speaking style had changed very little from his CSO days. He was not an emotional speaker. He convinced students to support the union through his sincerity, humility, and command of the facts about the struggle between the farm workers and the growers. His low-key approach was disarming in an age of radical and flamboyant rhetoric.

The national news media helped in generating support for the strike. Television news crews filmed the drama of the confrontations at the picket line. An NBC special, "The Harvest of Shame," depicted the tragic conditions of migrant laborers in the United States and helped to make people more aware of the farm workers' plight. Reporters from city newspapers and national magazines interviewed Chávez and other union officials as well as the growers. Chávez spoke about how the farm workers were fighting for their civil rights and economic justice. The farm worker movement dovetailed with the growing national concern about civil rights.

Publicity became increasingly important when the union launched a boycott to put pressure on the growers to recognize the union and sign contracts. They targeted the most iden-

Chávez speaking at a rally in the late 1960s. Photo by Chris Sanchez.

tifiable grape products from the largest Delano growers, the Schenley Corporation, the Di Giorgio Corporation, S and W Fine Foods, and TreeSweet. The success of the boycott depended on an informed and sympathetic consumer.

Early in the strike, national union leader Walter Reuther, head of the United Auto Workers, visited Delano (December 1965) and this brought national attention to the strike and boycott. Reuther was on the West Coast to attend the AFL–CIO midwinter convention in San Francisco and he had heard about the strike in Delano of Filipino and Mexican workers. For Reuther, the farm-labor movement reminded him of the labor militancy that the United Auto Workers had undertaken during the 1930s. With the urging of Paul Schrade, the UAW representative in California, he convinced the UAW to donate money to the strike. He traveled to Delano to present the check to Chávez and Al Green, the AWOC director. FWA and AWOC members met him at the airport and, in violation of the orders of the local police chief, prepared to stage a march through Delano to the union headquarters. Reuther held an FWA sign and marched next to Chávez and hundreds of supporters, surrounded by newspaper and television reporters who expected a confrontation. When they met the chief of police, the chief decided to back down. At the city hall, in front of the mayor and other dignitaries, Reuther gave a dramatic speech supporting the strike demands. Later, at Filipino Hall he held a press conference and, at César's request, agreed to meet with the growers to get them to settle the strike. Chávez later rated Reuther's support that day as the event that gave the grape strike its first wide national visibility.

THE MARCH ON SACRAMENTO

Other dramatic events gave momentum to the strike and boycott. Three months after Reuther's visit, on 16 March 1966, Chávez organized a march from Delano to Sacramento to dramatize the strike and get the support of California Governor Pat Brown. The march was a tactic Chávez had used with the CSO during the Oxnard struggle. Besides its practical political value, the march was linked to the idea of sacrifice. In Chávez's words, "This was an excellent way of training ourselves to endure the long, long struggle. . . . This was a penance more than anything else—and it was quite a penance, because there was an awful lot of suffering involved in this pilgrimage, a great deal of pain." In the spirit of the Lenten season, the march became a religious pilgrimage. It was planned to end on Easter Sunday, covering 250 miles in twenty-five days.

Chávez marched with the procession as it left Delano. Filipino, Mexican, African American, and Anglo members marched enthusiastically. They carried the U.S. and Mexican flags, the FWA and AWOC banners, and a flag with the image of the Virgin of Guadalupe. The march helped recruit more members and it spread the spirit of the strike. As they passed through the farming country of the San Joaquin Valley, at each small town hundreds of workers greeted them. Some joined the march and carried the flags to the next town. At night they had rallies with music, singing, speeches, and a dramatic reading of "El Plan de Delano" that Luis Valdez had composed in the spirit of Emiliano Zapata's "Plan de Ayala," a declaration of the agrarian revolution in 1910. The march generated spirit. The occupants of passing cars, if they supported the boycott and strike, would wave and honk; supporters of the growers would curse and make obscene gestures. By and large, there was local support, with hundreds of touching incidents. In one town a man and his daughters gave the marchers a drink of punch from a crystal bowl with cups. People working in the fields as the marchers passed by gave up their jobs and joined the procession.

For César, the Sacramento march was a painful ordeal. After the first couple of days his old shoes gave him blisters and one of his feet swelled considerably. Since he considered it a penitential walk, he refused to take medication to lessen the pain. By the end of the third day his leg was swollen and his blisters began to bleed. He was running a temperature. By the seventh day his physical condition was such that a nurse ordered him to ride in a station wagon for the rest of the march. He briefly rested in the station wagon, bitterly disappointed with himself. The next day he rejoined the marchers.

By the time the marchers reached Stockton, a few days from their goal, there were more than five thousand of them, singing, chanting, and waving as they walked. Chávez remembered: "People were getting in front of us with flowers. There were mariachis playing. It was a fiesta." That night in Stockton, Chávez got a phone call from Sidney Korshak, a representative of the Schenley Corporation. Korshak said, "I want to talk to you about recognizing the union and signing a contract." César thought it was a joke and hung up. But Korshak called back and they arranged a meeting in Beverly Hills the next day. After driving during the night to get there, César found himself in Korshak's home with Bill Kircher, the AFL–CIO's representative, and a Teamster representative. The Teamsters Union had helped the strikers by refusing to work Schenley's warehouse in San Francisco. Korshak said that Schenley was ready to sign a contract; the question was, with which union? Kirchner tried to pressure Chávez into letting AWOC get the contract, but César convinced Kirchner to compromise and let Schenley recognize the FWA and let AWOC be a signatory as a witness: that way, Kirchner could save face with his union. On 7 April the agreement was made public. In a triumphant mood, the pilgrimage ended a few days later on the steps of the state capitol. They had won their first victory and demonstrated the power of their cause. Governor Brown avoided meeting the marchers by going to Palm Springs to spend the weekend with Frank Sinatra: they held their celebration without him.

Schenley had been pressured into a contract by the FWA boycott. In particular, a rumor had been started that bartenders in New York were going to refuse to serve Schenley products in sympathy with the strike and this threat convinced the company to give in. For the first time in U.S. history, a grassroots, farm-labor union had gained recognition by a corporation (some years before, in Hawaii, the Longshoremen's Union had gotten a contract for pineapple workers).

DI GIORGIO, THE TEAMSTERS, AND A MERGER

Three days after the conclusion of the march, Chávez turned his attention to the largest grower in the Delano area, the Di Giorgio Corporation. Di Giorgio was a family-controlled company that had extensive holdings throughout California and Florida. The most important grape ranches that would become targets of the grape strike were located in Sierra Vista, Arvin, near Delano, and one ranch near Borrego Springs. The Di Giorgios also had thousands of acres of pears, plums, apricots, and citrus trees. They marketed their products under the S & W Fine Foods and TreeSweet labels. In 1965, the Di Giorgio Corporation netted $231 million. Robert Di Giorgio, the patriarch of the family, was on the board of directors of the Bank of America. The Di Giorgio family had successfully broken strikes and unions since the 1930s and Steinbeck, in his novel, *The Grapes of Wrath,* had used Di Giorgio as a model for the grower Gregorio.

Chávez was convinced of the power of the boycott and soon hundreds of volunteers who remembered previous struggles against the Di Giorgios joined the boycott drive. Within a short time the company agreed to enter into negotiations to have a union election, but Chávez broke off talks when company guards attacked a picketer at Sierra Vista. When negotiations resumed, Chávez discovered that Di Giorgio had invited the Teamsters to recruit members in the vineyards. He ended the negotiations in protest.

In California, New York, and the Midwest, Teamster locals had been supportive of the NFWA during the early months of the grape strike, but now the national Teamsters organization decided to organize farm workers to protect their members working as packers and as truckers. Almost one-fifth of all Teamster members worked in industries that were dependent on agriculture. The independent NFWA, with its strikes and boycotts, was a threat to the nonfield workers whose jobs depended on the harvest. In the parlance of labor organizers, the Teamsters entered the fields to "protect their flanks."

The Teamsters had helped break strikes before. In 1961 they had signed a "sweetheart" contract with Bud Antle, the largest grower of lettuce in California, to break a strike. This pattern seemed to be happening again. Beginning in mid-1966 the two unions, the Teamsters and the NFWA, began a jurisdictional fight that, on and off, lasted more than ten years, resulting in violence, injury, and several deaths.

Di Giorgio's strategy was to rush quickly into an election to determine union representation, having the assurance that the Teamsters would win. The Teamsters, in turn, would give him a contract which benefited the company. When Chávez learned of this move he rallied the union to boycott the elections, scheduled for 24 June: those who were on strike were not to be eligible to vote and essentially, only those who had already signed Teamster authorization cards would cast a ballot in favor of a union contract. The ensuing NFWA–AWOC boycott turned away almost half of the eligible voters and the union began lobbying the state governor to investigate the election and have it overturned. It was an election year, 1966, and Governor Brown was running against Ronald Reagan. He needed all the support he could get. Under pressure from the Mexican-American Political Association, lobbied by Dolores Huerta, Pat Brown agreed to launch an investigation, with the result, two weeks later, of a recommendation that the elections be invalidated and that a new election date be set for 30 August. Under the new agreement, any worker who had worked for Di Giorgio for fifteen days before the strike was eligible to vote, meaning that almost two thousand strikers would be able to cast their ballots.

Prior to the election, in 1966, to consolidate power AWOC and the NFWU formally merged to form a united union within the AFL-CIO. This move was not without controversy and danger. César was worried that within the AFL-CIO the union would be subject to regulations that would prohibit the boycott. Some of the student volunteers, especially the liberals and radicals, were very much opposed to merging their movement with organized labor. César's staff split on the issue. Marshall Ganz, a Harvard-educated civil rights worker in charge of the international boycott, was in favor of the merger. Jim Drake, Chávez's adviser, was against it. The migrant ministry staff supported it. César realized that the rank and file had to be educated to the benefits of the merger before they would agree. With about a month left before the 30 August election, César decided to ask for a vote and not a single farm worker voted against the reorganization.

Under the merger agreement, a new organization, called the United Farm Workers Organizing Committee (UFWOC— eventually to become the United Farm Workers of America, AFL-CIO) was formed, with Chávez as the director. The new organization continued with strategies of the older NFWA. When the AWOC staff learned that their salaries were going to be reduced and that they would have to give up their plush expense accounts, they resigned (an exception was Larry Itliong). Chávez explained his philosophy of leadership to the new staff: "The job can't be done unless there is a commitment. If we're going to lead people and ask them to starve and really sacrifice, we've got to do it first, do it more than anybody else, because it isn't the orders, it isn't the pronouncements, it's the deeds that count."

With the merger, the new UFWOC became truly a multiethnic union. Most of the AWOC members were Filipino, and most of the NFWA were Mexican. César had to argue against those who wanted to keep the union controled by Mexicans. César told them that the Filipinos had to be represented in all the union activities and services. Most of the Mexicans went along with the integration of leadership and services, but a few were ready to quit the union in protest. From the beginning, César had not thought of La Causa as a movement that would be motivated primarily by appeals to race or nationality. When César had worked for the CSO, he had confronted the issue of Mexican chauvinism and had been uncompromising in fighting for the inclusion of blacks within the organization. Although the core leadership of the NFWA was Mexican-American, the staff and hundreds of volunteer workers were predominantly Anglo.

The merger strategy paid off with an election victory at Di Giorgio's farms. The UFWOC volunteers had worked arduously to round up former employees of the company and migrant families who had heard of the impending elections traveled from as far as central Mexico to cast their ballots. On election day, the union ran a shuttle service to pick up workers to take them to the polling place. The next day, supervised by the arbitration association, they counted the ballots in San Francisco: UFWOC had won, getting 530 votes to the Teamsters' 331. Only 12 workers voted to not have a union. That day there was a hugh celebration in Filipino Hall in Delano, but there still remained the problem of negotiating a satisfactory contract with Di Giorgio. The boycott would continue for another four years, when a contract was signed. At least for now, victory was sweet.

Shortly after the victory, César received a congratulatory telegram from Dr. Martin Luther King Jr. In part King said, "You and your valiant fellow workers have demonstrated your commitment to righting grievous wrongs forced upon exploited people. We are together with you in spirit and in determination that our dreams for a better tomorrow will be realized."

But in August 1966, the "dreams of a better tomorrow" were beginning to look like nightmares. The civil rights movement, so full of promise a year earlier, was taking a violent turn. That summer, bloody race riots erupted in major U.S. cities. The philosophy of nonviolence was being denounced by new black militants: Stokely Carmichael and H. Rap Brown in the Student Nonviolent Coordinating Committee; and Bobby Seale and Huey Newton of the Black Panther movement. Malcolm X, too, leader of the Black Muslims who was assassinated in 1965, also had not looked kindly on nonviolence. On campuses, the opposition to the war in Vietnam and racism became more vocal. Students organized peace marches and teach-ins, burned draft cards, and demonstrated against ROTC and military recruiters.

Meanwhile, a nationwide Chicano movement was beginning to take shape with La Causa at the forefront. In New Mexico, a fiery Baptist preacher, Reies López Tijerina, had organized Hispanos to regain the lands they had lost after the American takeover in 1848. The Alianza Federal de Mercedes Libres, established in 1963, claimed more than twenty thou-

sand members. Under Tijerina's leadership the alliance began
to be more militant in its tactics. In July 1966 they had organized a march of sixty-two miles from Albuquerque to Santa
Fe to demand that the state government investigate the theft
of land grants. Within a few months, Tijerina and his followers
occupied federal lands and declared an independent Hispano
nation, the Republic of San Joaquín del Rio de Chama.

In Colorado, a former middleweight boxing champion, Rudolfo "Corky" Gonzales, in 1966 founded the Denver Crusade
for Justice, a civil rights group dedicated to the promotion of
Chicano liberation and nationalism. Gonzales appealed to the
urban barrios in his attacks on the inadequacies of the school
system and police brutality. His epic poem, *I Am Joaquín*, was
an inspirational message calling for a reaffirmation of identity
and pride. Like Luis Valdez with his Centro Campesino, Gonzales established a cultural center that functioned as an alternative school, La Escuela de Tlatelolco, La Plaza de las Tres
Culturas. Unlike Chávez and the UFWOC, Gonzales appealed
to Chicano ethnic consciousness to form a Chicano nation.

Thus, by the end of 1966 Chávez and the farm workers were
part of a broad-based, nationally known movement. La Causa
of the farm workers became part of the agenda for scores of
local Chicano movement organizations. The UFW black eagle
appeared at almost every Chicano rally and would become an
icon of the Chicano movement. Chávez's leadership had gal-
vanized widespread support beyond the Mexican-American
communities, including student radicals, liberals, clerics, and
organized labor. Together they had produced some limited
victories, but the conflict was far from over. In some respects,
it was just beginning.

CHAPTER 4

Coleadership: The Strength of Dolores Huerta

I am visible—see this Indian face—
yet I am invisible.
To survive the Borderlands/You must live
sin fronteras/*be a crossroads.*

GLORIA ANZALDUA

BY 1966, César Chávez and Dolores Huerta had a symbiotic relationship. Chávez was the visible leader and Huerta was the "hidden" one. He functioned as the catalyst; she was the engine. Most people did not realize the qualities Huerta brought to the Farm Workers Association: personal strength, communication skills, an ethic of work, an intellectual approach, and a strong sense of self. In 1962, Chávez had asked Huerta to be cofounder of the Farm Workers Association because he recognized her leadership abilities, her powerful character, her intellectual toughness, and above all her self-assuredness. Farm workers listened to her; young Chicanas followed her. She placed the traces of her character on the union, just as Chávez placed the traces of his spirit, his soul, on the union. To understand Chávez and the union, we must also understand Huerta.

Her role in shaping César Chávez's life and the farm-worker movement was crucial, especially during the early organizational years. To the farm workers she was La Pasionaria (the Passionate One) and a union leader. To César she was a key negotiator, a nontraditional Mexicana, and a loyal follower. While many books have been written about César Chávez (see

Bibliographic Essay), almost nothing has been written about Huerta. Her appearance is familiar, but not her persona. She is a woman, an organizer, and a symbol of justice and fairness, and she carries the aura of César Chávez and the United Farm Workers Union. During her adult life, she was the organizer who led the Chávez negotiating team against the powerful growers. She worked as a lobbyist for the union in Washington and Sacramento; and she innovated in using the management theories of Kenneth Blanchard to restructure the farm workers' union into an almost corporate-like structure. More than once she has risked her life for Chávez and the union.

Dolores Huerta has been an important influence on Chávez and the union. Like Chávez she has been a follower of Saul Alinsky's basic belief that the poor must determine their own issues and that a mass organizational drive for power is basic. Huerta has not been driven by ideological concerns but by a passion for justice and fairness. But she functioned like a corporate executive. To understand the inner strengths of the union is to understand the strength, drive, and the many personalities of Huerta.

CRITICISMS

Dolores Huerta is a very complicated woman. She was often at odds with César. As she has said: "César and I have a lot of personal fights, usually over strategy or personalities. I don't think César himself understands why he fights with me." Judith Coburn, writing in *Ms. Magazine,* said that "a book could be written on their complex relationship." Both were stubborn and opinionated, and Dolores was notorious in the union for her combativeness. She also has had frequent conflict with her two husbands—the price of a strong personality and her independence. For example, Dolores forced Ventura Huerta, her second husband, to quit his job and work with her in union activities because she was not being accepted as an organizer in the first few years. He would "front" for her as the organizer while she made the decisions. Ventura vigorously opposed her methods and also disagreed with Huerta's belief that family came second to her work in the union. Dolores's father opposed her "unconventional family and personal life."

Perhaps it is because of her independence and strong personality: Dolores has had two husbands and presently maintains a live-in arrangement with Richard Chávez, César's older brother. During these three relationships, she has borne eleven children, bringing responsibilities that have not compromised her union activity. As she acknowledges, "The time I spend with my kids is very limited." Sometimes she is separated for months at a time from her children. As several writers have pointed out, she is a tough, competitive, individualistic, and very skilled woman. Because of her conflicts with men, her "neglect" of her children, and her aggressive role in the union many traditionalist Mexican women have berated her, although young Chicanas were attracted to her independent stand. In many ways, Huerta lives in the space between the traditional woman's role and the radical feminist one.

Huerta resembles the New Mestiza—a role Gloria Anzaldua describes in her book, *Borderlands/La Frontera*, living on the border between tradition and nontradition, between the accepted and the unacceptable. As Anzaldua puts it: "Living on borders and in margins, deepening in fact one's shifting and multiple identity and integrity, is like trying to swim in a new element, an alien element." Many Mexican women, in addition to criticizing her conflict with men and her aggressive, almost manlike role in the union, berate Huerta for "neglect" of her children. At times, César Chávez, reacting to her independent personality, even said to her: "You're not a Mexican." She has replied: "I know it's true, I am a logical person. I went to school, and you learn that you have to weigh both sides and look at things objectively." Chávez is more dogmatic in his views than Huerta. She is able to move pragmatically through the limits of "lo Mexicano" and "lo Americano" without losing her sense of both.

Thus, Huerta diverges from the traditionally accepted model of the Mexican woman, especially women like César Chávez's wife Helen. Writing of this comparison, historian Margaret Rose has concluded that Huerta is a very nontraditional woman who is unlike the majority of strong Mexican women, who are not combative or competitive. Within accepted Mexican tradition, a woman, according to Rose, may be an activist, but she must still be a housewife. She can be an organizer, but not a leader. Rose writes that "Huerta's union activism is atypical. She rebelled against the conventional constraints upon women's full participation in trade union activism, competing directly with male colleagues in the UFW." Rose also writes that Huerta's "activism resembles that of other well-known Latina labor leaders of earlier generations, such as Emma Tenayuca and Luisa Moreno: it can only be labeled 'non-traditional.'" For Rose, the more traditional activist is Helen Chávez, because she "juggles" not sidesteps the "demands of family life," the sexual division of labor, and quietly protests behind her man. Huerta does not think of herself simply as a woman; nor does she conduct her life vis-à-vis men as did 1945 labor activist Josefina Fierro de Bright. She is different. She simply sees her work as a personal calling rather than as a woman's duty to her man—or allegiance to ideological fervor, which was the case with both Moreno and Tenayuca.

AN EGALITARIAN UPBRINGING

Huerta's upbringing shaped her attitudes toward gender: her inner strength and independent resourcefulness comes from her mother. As Huerta recalled in an interview, "My mother raised me and was a dominant figure in my early years. At home, we all shared equally in the household tasks. I never had to cook for my brothers or do their clothes like many traditional Mexican families." Writer Ruth Carranza further suggests that "Huerta's egalitarian family background has contributed to her leadership style. For Huerta there was no sexual discrimination in her home and consequently no sense of inferiority or no encouragement to accept a sense of secondary role in her life and later in her work with the union. Also, there was no contradictory masculine/feminine messages by her mother."

Consequently, Huerta's assertiveness is predicated on her strong sense of self. This character trait is what is appealing to farm-worker women, to urban Mexican-American women, and to young Chicanas. It is her air of personal strength, of assertiveness, her disdain of feminine mystique that caused long-time organizer and labor leader Bert Corona to call her too aggressive. Corona liked the fieriness of Luisa Moreno and the sexuality of Josefina Fierro de Bright. Unlike these other women leaders, Huerta helped Chávez and the union by being a role model for young Chicanas.

Ironically, though Huerta in her family life and her organizational work is the "new woman" that the younger generation seems to be seeking, she has acted publicly as if she were the traditional woman behind the male leader Chávez. Chávez tried to keep a tight rein on his lieutenants, even on his equals like Huerta. But Dolores Huerta, by her strong, everyday example, broke from the image of the traditional mother and wife and the role of the traditional woman activist behind the scenes. Her behavior toward Chávez and other male farm workers helped to break gender and sexual misperceptions of women. This allowed for equality within the union. Again, she exemplifies what Anzaldua has written of the New Mestiza: "To live in the borderlands means you are neither hispana, india, negra, española, ni gabacha, eres mestiza, mulata, half-breed caught in the crossfire between camps while carrying all five races on your back not knowing which side to turn to, run from; to survive the Borderlands you must live sin fronteras, be a crossroads." Huerta as a woman lives at these crossroads of gender and ethnicity.

Huerta began to experience this life *sin fronteras* (without borders) as a child. She grew up assuming that women and men were equal because she constantly saw the strength and activism of her mother—a business entrepreneur, independent of men. She also saw and accepted the ideal of equality in a part of the United States where ethnicity was not a barrier. As she writes: "I was raised with two brothers and a mother, so there was no sexism. My mother was a strong woman and she did not favor my brothers. There was no idea that men were superior. I was also raised in Stockton in an integrated neighborhood. There were Chinese, Latinos, Native Americans, Blacks, Japanese, Italians, and others. We were all rather poor, but it was an integrated community so it was not racist for me in my childhood." Huerta perceived and interpreted the world as one of equality between men and women, regardless of ethnicity. She felt free to be herself and worked hard to succeed in school. She believed that she could participate in life as actively as her mother had. She especially saw how her mother, after her first divorce, had, without the help of a man, worked hard and started a successful restaurant and a hotel.

Her mother provided Dolores with a semblance of middle-class life, in values if not in fact. She gave Dolores both personal security and the financial foundation to pursue her education in an integrated high school and continue her education at a community college. As a result, Huerta grew up being active in the Girl Scouts, singing in a church choir, and aspiring to be a dancer. She learned the value of work, hope, perseverance, and independence. Huerta describes her mother as independent, ambitious, and a "Mexican-American Horatio Alger type." Her mother was her model, the United States was her teacher, and men were simply other people, not superiors, not bosses. Above all, Huerta saw herself and her friends as proof that Chicanos could succeed in the United States. She remembers that "all the Chicanos who went to school where I did are all making it. We grew up in Stockton, but weren't in a ghetto. As a result, we didn't have a whole bunch of hang-ups, like hating Anglos, or hating Blacks."

Clearly, Huerta grew up in a communal atmosphere of security and self-esteem, where ethnic differences were not insuperable barriers. Like Emma Tenayuca, she grew up with a middle-class mentality. She reflected such values of stability, tradition, and "Americanism" that, in her twenties, she briefly joined the Republican Party. In fact, her Americanism was so pronounced that, as she remembers, "I thought Fred Ross from the Community Service Organization . . . a Sal Alinsky organizer, was a Communist, so I went to the FBI and had him checked out. I really did that. I used to work for the Sheriff's Department. See how middle class I was. In fact, I was a registered Republican at the time [the late fifties]." However, in spite of her middle-class life, she remembers having friends who were pachucos and says: "I don't think I was ever really a cop-out."

But her life had many moments of ambiguity. For example, she later recollected that in elementary school the equality she had felt was tainted. "The teachers," she remembers, "treated us all equally mean." Later, in high school, underneath the world of lessons, A-grades, and clubs, there lurked a world of clear difference between rich and poor. "When I got into high school," she writes, "it was really segregated. There were the real rich and the real poor. I later realized we were poor too, and I had got hit with a lot of racial discrimination." In spite of the racism, Huerta succeeded, but she was frustrated. As she yearned to succeed in college, she continued to notice the inequalities. She saw the poor on the streets and realized that most of the out-crowd of her high school clubs were "poor," too. She specifically remembers being crushed—her word— when she was questioned on the legitimacy of her high school essays, since they were so well written. The teacher thought someone else was writing them for her. "That really discouraged me," she said, "because I used to stay up all night and think, and try to make every paper different, and try to put words in there that I thought were nice."

Huerta consequently began to see life through a different lens, not because she felt an absence of freedom, or because of a personal sense of inequality, but because of widespread injustice—which applied to her, her Mexican friends, and other Americans. In short, she began to see the paradox between equality and justice, and equality and class. These disparities became more apparent to her after her mother took her, at age seventeen, to Mexico City. "This trip," she recalls, "opened my eyes to that fact that there was nothing wrong with Chicanos." The contrasts between Mexican and United States society made her acutely aware of two realities: societal injustices and her own lack of activism.

She remembered the other side of her mother's personality: her mother's commitment to helping poor Mexicano families; and she also felt her New Mexico traditions of Hispanidad. She became active in women's Hispanic groups, such as the Comité Honorífico Women's Club. She pursued the traditional elite Mexican woman's activist role: to serve in women's organizations, apart from men. But she soon discovered that "all of these organizations . . . didn't do anything but give dances and celebrate the Fiestas Patrias." This demonstration of civic virtue in the women's world did not satisfy her.

Simultaneously, her first marriage (in 1950 she had married an Irishman—her high school sweetheart) was failing and she found her role as a mother to several children to be unsatisfying. She also found that her two years of college no longer provided her with adequate intellectual or personal satisfaction. As she writes: "I felt I had all of these frustrations inside me. I had a fantastic complex because I seemed to be out of step with everybody and everything. You're trying to go to school and yet you see all of these injustices. It was just such a complex." Even teaching, in the 1950s, and helping children did not satisfy her. However, her awareness of racism, poverty, inequality, and discrimination inflicted on the poor had not yet replaced her middle-class life: she was caught in her own world of children, motherhood, and wifely dependence; caught in the central tension of her life—between dreams of education and achievement on one hand and an acute awareness of injustice and unfairness on the other. Remembering her mother's constant advice—which would become an axiom—"Be yourself," she began to shift her view to a new life perspective—a new gestalt.

"BE YOURSELF"

In 1955, armed with a community college background (which was more education than most women had in the 1950s) and good bilingual skills, she began actively to change her life. She was driven by a strong belief that she *could* change her life; and the lives of others. Hearing Saul Alinsky's call for radicalism in the voice of Fred Ross, she joined the Community Service Organization. As she would later say, she put herself at the service of others as an organizer and negotiator. As she entered the man's world of the 1950s, she held to an important belief: that, in any endeavor, "women have one advantage over men, their egos aren't so involved." She could *"Be herself"* and serve without feeling threatened by men. As she put it: "I think women are particularly good negotiators and organizers because we have a lot of patience, and no ego trips to overcome." She thus entered the world of power. The message from the Saul Alinsky Industrial Areas Foundation and the CSO was to gain reform for the poor by actively involving them in achieving reform—and the emphasis of Alinsky's message coincided with hers: a pragmatic, nonideological approach to life and change.

The world of the CSO and later the farm-workers union was no different from any other sector of the business or corporate world: they all needed good organizing executive managers who wanted to succeed. Dolores Huerta fit this description. She was free of a sense of ethnic inferiority—a woman who felt equal to men in a world where women were still considered to be the second sex.

THE ORGANIZER: "PURSUING JUSTICE"

Dolores Huerta responded to Fred Ross's CSO in 1955 about her becoming an organizer because the job provided her with both an avenue to serve the poor and an avenue to "make

it"—albeit not in mainstream America. The new challenge coincided with her philosophical axiom: "Be yourself." As she
put it: "I like to organize and help people. I like social change.
I feel humble because I've been very fortunate in my life. God
has put me in the position and provided the opportunities and
skills to get things done." In following a life of service, Huerta
was making personal, moral, and political choices.

Huerta never changed her mind about her decision. She
endured the criticism of her father (for failing in her wifely
and motherly duties); she suffered through two failed mar-
riages; she became the target of the anger of both middle-class
and farm-working women (who berated her for neglecting
her children, although she entrusted them to communal parents when she went on months-long organizing trips); and
she endured the resentment of male farm workers and put up
with Chávez's constant anger at her independence. Above all,
she endured conditions of poverty for herself and her children: she often did not have money for milk or food. In 1962,
she moved from a relatively comfortable administrative position with the Community Service Organization to work as
the powerful, but still impoverished, first vice-president and
principal director of negotiations for the farmworkers organizing committee. Jean Murphy, writing in *Regeneracion,* put
Huerta's notable role and difficult choice in clear perspective:

> If César Chávez is the hero of the Farmworkers movement, Do-
> lores Huerta is its unheralded heroine. Huerta plays a key orga-
> nizing and leadership role. The role, however, is not easy. Eigh-
> teen hour days of planning boycotts, of speaking at rallies, of
> negotiating, of traveling, and of seeking public support for La
> Causa are more common than not. Nor is the work well paid.
> Like all other union officials and employees, she makes a minimal
> salary and a bare subsistence depending upon contributions of
> food and clothing. In her own humorous words Huerta has said
> of her choice: "All of us have very exotic wardrobes. We get our
> clothes out of donations."

Huerta's egalitarianism and sense of justice also seem to be
taken from America's trashcan. Out of discards she has fash-

ioned a sense of hope and leadership, a hope based on the conviction that justice and fairness are the intellectual basis for a new society. As an organizer, Huerta still carries with her memories of youthful anomalies: the selfless elementary school girl selling war bonds; the girl working overtime to write papers that were considered suspect because they were written too well; the child watching her mother help farm workers and braceros; the girl writing poems to capture a more sensitive world; or the teenager fighting for lower ticket prices to help the poor at high school.

Her early experiences have helped shape her guiding manifesto as she seeks to balance differences between rich and poor. In the choices she made to establish a new life, Huerta took a pragmatic approach to her moral conflict. Her ideas were implicit guides to activity and behavior; and her knowledge of what was good and right was verified by her activism. She did not attempt intellectually to resolve her frustrations, her unorthodoxy, and her moral crisis. Stressing the power of moral choice, Huerta applied it to her work as an organizer and leader. She believes that the power for change is predicated on the power of individuals to make moral choices for justice over personal welfare. For Huerta, all individuals—farm workers, academics, and everyone else—must make a commitment, and the totality of commitment will either form a mass organization or establish a climate for a political movement.

Huerta believes that organizing is a creative process that gives her intellectual and personal fulfillment. She says: "My duties are policy-making like [those of] César Chávez. It is the creative part of the organization. I am in charge of political and legislative activity. Much of my work is in public relations." All her work, regardless of whether it is policymaking, political and legislative activity, or public relations, is always based on four axioms: first, to establish a strong sense of identity; second, to develop a sense of pride; third, always to maintain the value of service to others; and fourth, to be self-reflective and true to oneself. For Huerta, all organizing and leadership work must be imbued with these principles. When Huerta described what she wanted her children to become, she summarized her major ideals: "Tough, political, responsible, and loving." Above all, she believes in psychological strength. She has always urged the Mexican community, the politician, and the poor in general not to be afraid to deal with issues. As she put it, *"que no fueran miedosos"* (do not be afraid of anything).

Huerta has remained selfless as an organizer, committed to a philosophy of service that she has pragmatically developed. Luis Valdez, artist, producer, and former head of the farm workers' teatro, perceptively captured Huerta's qualities as a woman and organizer in a 1990 newspaper article:

> Dolores was a 35 year old firebrand in 1965, and she was commanding crusty macho campesinos 20 years her senior. What dazzled my radicalized university-trained Chicano mind was that she led through persuasion and personal example, rather than intimidation, and that she was one hell of an organizer. People tend to forget that the 1960s were the sexist dark ages, even in the Chicano movement, as we called it, but Dolores was already way out in front. She was a woman, a Mexican-American, a Chicana cutting a swath of revolutionary action across the torpidity of the San Joaquin Valley.

Valdez adds: "The wonder of Dolores Huerta is that she has never given up struggling for what is right, decent and human in the world, and she never will."

This strong will and consciousness of egalitarianism are the underlying factors that maintain Huerta's sense of hope. They also established her style of intellectual leadership. As Huerta says: "To me a leader is someone who does things for people and whom people will follow. It is not somebody who gets out there and imposes himself on people. I think people develop charisma in trying to reach people, in trying to get to them. Gradually and before you know it, you become a charismatic leader." Like Chávez, Huerta feels that a leader should get commitment from the workers—commitment to service for their own goals.

HUERTA'S IDEAS

Through her early organizing years, Huerta did not consider herself to be a feminist or Chicana leader: she just followed her assumptions that equality is basic to life, and that justice, fairness, is the key. "I have been asked," she says,

> whether being a woman has made it difficult for me in my exercise of leadership. For years I never thought about that. We were too busy in organizing struggles. Now suddenly I am invited to speak here and there on different issues. The suggestion being that I am a symbol of the women's movement or that I speak for Hispanic women. And that has been difficult, I am a sort of born again feminist.

In spite of this recent consciousness of feminism, she has always realized the importance of women in building the union, and of there being strong and independent women leaders and organizers. "I know," she says," that the history of our union would have been quite different had it not been for my involvement. So I am trying to get more of our women to hang in there. The energy of women is important." Huerta speaks these strong words for female leadership without overlooking the importance of male leadership in organization too.

She believes that the equal participation of women in an organization is vital. "The participation of women has helped keep the movement nonviolent," she says. For Huerta, women are more patient, less volatile than men. For Chávez the philosophical ideal on gender was for women to be separate but equal; for Huerta, women's leadership complemented men's, and therefore gender equality and justice were not only to be pursued as goals but they must be nurtured and practiced in daily organizing activities. Equality, for Huerta, is intertwined with justice and gender, but the core of her philosophy remains the freedom of self through choice.

Dolores Huerta's ideas are rooted in numerous traditions. In many ways her conceptualization, "Be yourself," is very American, echoing the traditions of Emerson and Thoreau; that is, she stresses individual freedom and morality but ties them to communal responsibility. These notions were also espoused by the Mexican-American intellectual Octavio Romano in his 1960s and 1970s journal, *El Grito*. In addition, her emphasis of the idea that organizers and leaders do not just give to the workers in the tradition of liberal-welfarism, or lead in the Marxist-Leninist tradition, coincides with Saul Alinsky's philosophy of organizing. Knowingly or not, she also mirrors John Rawls's idea that justice conveys a philosophical core of individual inviolability, a doctrine of fairness, and a method of compromise. Consequently, Huerta's simple message can function to deconstruct the utilitarian philosophy of justice that operates in the United States, calling for the greatest good for the greatest number. Huerta wants the poor to sit side by side with the rich and contractually agree to the choices of the primary goods and services to be distributed (i.e., liberties; economic, personal, intellectual, and political freedoms).

Huerta argues that there is a need for "mass organizations," "voter registration," "voter education," and for the people themselves to "identify the issues." "Our success," she continues, "is due to the New Deal tradition among older Americans" and the "younger generation which responds to César's charismatic leadership." Huerta clearly links the New Deal policies of justice and fairness with the 1960s youth rebellion for a new, Hobbesian contractualism and redistribution of society's primary goods and services.

While César Chávez was more directly concerned with building a union and getting people's commitment to such specific union activities as boycotts, Huerta was not always directly attempting to build a commitment to the farm workers' union. She supported other causes, too. She reaches out to people with a simple message that can shape an alternative intellectual world. It is not an ideological message; nor is she calling for a structural revolution: she is simply demanding a new moral commitment based on a new sense of individual responsibility. Her vision of justice calls for this alternative intellectual world to be used as an ideal plan of action. Her thought is within the philosophical tradition of pragmatic self-discovery. For Huerta, ideas, action, and the individual are central to change, and gender is a core strength and energy. In her words: "The worst thing that I see is guys who say, 'man, they don't have any Chicanos up there [in places of power'], and they're not in there working to make sure that it happens. We [as Chicanos] criticize and separate ourselves from the process of change. We've got to jump in there with both feet to change conditions." For Huerta, ideas are vital, criticism is necessary—but it is action, through a responsible commitment and moral choice, that is the key to creating a just society.

A SYMBOL OF OPENNESS

As outlined above, Huerta represents many different ideas, but she always illustrates the ideas of fairness and justice, regardless of her audience. Because of this perception of her openness, César Chávez does not see her as he sees himself, strong and unwavering on certain ideas and ideals. Huerta points out that Chávez often referred to her as a "liberal." She once said: "When he really wants to get me mad he says, 'you're not a Mexican,' because he says I have liberal hangups. And I know it's true. I am a logical person. I went to school and you learn that you have to weigh both sides and look at things objectively. But the farm workers, I believe, know that wrong is wrong. They know that there's evil in the world and that you have to fight evil."

Clearly, Huerta is more than just a unionist, an ethnic representative, or a liberal. We cannot rely on the familiar categories to characterize or understand Huerta. Although all of these, she retains her own distinctiveness. She exhibits all the personal and symbolic attributes applied to her—feminist, na-

Dolores Huerta on mike. Her T-shirt dates the photo as being from the Gallo strike in 1973.

tionalist, humble, aggressive, nontraditional, and passionate. But her individuality is in their overlapping and their excesses as she responds to events and issues. It is difficult to place Huerta within one intellectual tradition because she works with the constantly changing material of issues and crises as determined by people in different communities. She is continuously revitalized by, as well as revitalizing, temporal issues and discursive events.

Unlike other Latina women organizers such as Emma Tenayuca, Luisa Moreno, or Josefina Fierro de Bright, Huerta functions in her own space—a space at the crossroads of liberalism, conservatism, and radicalism. She speaks when others are still silent. For example, in April 1973, at the height of the nationalist and ethnocentric Chicano movement, when nothing short of ideological purity was the required litmus test for all Chicanos, Dolores Huerta attended the seventy-fifth birthday of Paul Robeson, joining the likes of Angela Davis, Pete Seeger, Ramsey Clark, James Earl Jones, Ossie Davis, Sidney Poitier, Harry Belafonte, Mayor Richard G. Hatcher, Coretta Scott King, and multitudes of others who jammed Carnegie Hall. She joined in supporting Robeson's message, "dedicated to the worldwide cause of humanity," especially when she linked Robeson's humanism and universalism to the cause of the farm workers under the grito of "Viva Robeson! Viva la causa!"

At its core, then, Huerta's cause is societal openness, universal equality, and a new humanism based on justice. Obviously, Huerta is a symbol of openness—of not fixing knowledge to truths, of not dogmatizing life, of not establishing barriers by ethnicity. For her, justice is at the crossroads of freedom and equality. As she stated, "I would like to be remembered as a woman who cares for fellow humans. We must use our lives to make the world a better place to live, not just to acquire things. That is what we are put on the earth for." This simple but fundamentally radical message mirrors that of Chávez— that everyone should make a personal moral choice of commitment to and responsibility for justice.

CHAPTER 5

Courage and Persistence

*I am convinced that the truest act of courage, the strongest
act of manliness, is to sacrifice ourselves for others in a totally
nonviolent struggle for justice. To be a man is to suffer for others.
God help us to be men!*

CÉSAR CHÁVEZ

BETWEEN 1965 and 1970 the UFW (in 1965 it was the NFWA)
grew in strength, nourished by the support of millions of sympathetic Americans whose social conscience had been aroused
by the farm workers' struggle. Hundreds of volunteers lived on
poverty wages in the large cities, organizing an international
boycott of table grapes to try to force the growers to negotiate
with the union. Scores of priests, nuns, ministers, and church
members donated time, money, facilities, and energies to the
farm workers' cause. Organized labor donated money to the
UFW strike fund and volunteers to work on the boycott.
Millions of Americans gave up eating table grapes. This new
national consciousness was inspired by the example of César
Chávez, the soft-spoken, unassuming leader who quietly worked
to revolutionize grower-worker relations.

At the same time as the UFW campaign was growing, there
were indications of a political awakening among Mexican-
Americans in the Southwest. Leaders emerged who addressed
the pressing economic and social issues that confronted the
growing millions of people of Mexican descent. In Texas, a
young student, José Angel Gutiérrez, organized a new political party, La Raza Unida, to try to push for Chicano representation within the system. Other more militant leaders like
Tijerina and Corky Gonzales also inspired a new activism.

Protests and confrontations between urban Mexican Americans and representatives of the schools, the police, and the churches became more frequent, especially after 1968. César Chávez and the UFW became an inspiring example of the emerging power of Mexican Americans within the United States. This power, however, was not to be easily won or permanently recognized.

TEXAS AND THE TEAMSTERS

Soon after the first Di Giorgio "election," in 1966, Chávez and Bill Kircher, the national organizing director for the AFL-CIO, flew to Texas to participate in a march that had been organized by several UFW staff members and local Tejanos. At the time, the Texas melon workers were considering a merger of their organization, the Independent Workers Association, with Chávez's union. The march was to protest the abysmal wages and degraded living conditions endured by the South Texas farm workers, who earned less than $1.00 an hour (California workers earned almost twice as much). They modeled their march after the famous Delano-to-Sacramento pilgrimage of earlier that year, planning to travel 450 miles from Rio Grande City to Austin, the state capital. Almost ten thousand people joined the procession by the time it reached Austin. On the capitol steps, Chávez gave the marchers strong words of encouragement and promised that the UFW would do all it could to support them. Before the rally began, Texas Governor John Connally told the marchers that he would not meet their demand to convene a special session of the legislature to enact a minimum-wage law. It looked like it would be a long struggle.

After the march César and Kircher went to Rio Grande City to explore the possibilities of extending their organizations to Texas. After they left, in August 1966, the Independent Workers Association members voted to merge with the newly united UFW. Antonio Orendain, who had worked with César in Delano, was put in charge of the Texas organization.

For the next eight years he struggled to build the farm workers' union there until political and personal difficulties forced him to leave the UFW in 1975 and form an independent organization, the Texas Farm Workers Union.

After the Rio Grande City meeting, César flew to Miami to give a speech to an electrical workers' convention and to seek their support for the California boycott. From there he flew to Mexico City to meet with Mexican labor union officials to ask their cooperation in stopping strikebreakers. It would not be the last meeting of Chávez with Mexican labor officials and high-level members of the Mexican government. The UFW had a common interest with Mexican labor unions in attempting to raise wages and in promoting worker solidarity during strikes. The Mexican government, for its part, shared UFW's interest in protecting the labor rights of Mexican nationals in the United States.

Back in California, the struggle with the Teamsters Union continued through the remainder of 1966 and into the summer of 1967. A few weeks after winning the Di Giorgio election on 30 August 1966, César turned his attention to a strike that union members voted for at the Perelli-Minetti vineyards. He soon found out that Perelli-Minetti had signed a sweetheart contract with the Teamsters as a way of breaking the strike. For the next several months, César devoted his full energies to forcing Perelli-Minetti to rescind its Teamster connections and recognize the UFW. It was a straightforward matter of not setting a bad precedent. Said Chávez: "We felt that if we didn't fight now, every time we got our grower ready to sign, he would go to the Teamsters." For eleven months, Chávez pushed for a boycott of all Perelli-Minetti products, targeting their wines and vermouth. Because of the label identification on the bottles, the boycott was quickly successful in forcing the company to get the Teamsters to settle with Chávez. At a hastily called meeting with César, Bill Grami, in charge of Teamster agricultural organization, signed

Chávez speaking at a rally. The aim was to get shoppers to boycott grapes.

a no-raiding jurisdictional pact, agreeing to withdraw from the vineyards. Perelli-Minetti gave the Teamster contract to the UFW.

It was during these negotiations that César went on the first of what would be many fasts. He had been praying for a satisfactory resolution to the talks and, when victory appeared imminent, he had decided to observe a fast of thanksgiving. The purpose of the fast changed, however, when the negotiations stalled. It was now undertaken as a protest. As with his later fasts, César did not tell anyone that he was fasting at first. He just continued his normal work routine as the negotiations continued. Later, friends and family found out that he was on a fast. After thirteen days he was a physical and mental wreck and he had to stay in bed for a couple of days to recover. He knew very little about the effects of fasting and how to prepare for it mentally. Later he would learn some of the spiritual and physical techniques that Gandhi and others had used during their fasts.

THE USE OF UNDOCUMENTED IMMIGRANTS

In 1967, the union moved from its cramped offices on Albany Street, Delano, to new buildings on land they had purchased with the help of private donations and contributions from AFL-CIO affiliates. The new headquarters was located near the city dump on 40 acres of alkali land. Volunteers had erected a complex of buildings, including a service and administrative center, a medical clinic, and a cooperative gas station. Named "The Forty Acres," it became the center of the farm workers' union movement in California for three years, after which time the union moved its headquarters to Keene, a small town outside Bakersfield.

On 1 April 1967, the UFW signed a contract with Di Giorgio Fruit Corporation. The contract contained wage increases for workers and set up a fund for health and welfare benefits. It provided for unemployment compensation and specified that hiring would be done through the union labor-hall. But the contract was with only one grower and UFW strikes continued against other Delano growers. By October, seven more wineries had signed contracts with the union. But with these limited successes, César was unhappy. The piecemeal approach to getting contracts with the growers was wearing and expensive for the union: it would be decades before the whole grape growing industry would be unionized. What was needed was a larger effort.

The opportunity for this effort presented itself when the workers at Giumarra, the largest table-grape grower in Delano, voted to strike. The Giumarra Corporation controlled more than 11,000 acres of vineyards and grossed $5 to $7½ million a year. It was family owned and run, a corporation led by Joseph Giumarra, a feisty seventy-year-old Italian immigrant who had built his empire by hard work, sacrifice, and the use of government subsidized water. Joe Giumarra was from the old school of agriculture, fiercely opposing union-ization. Along with his nephew John Giumarra, a young law-yer, he mounted a public relations campaign to combat the UFW strike.

The main arena of conflict early in the strike was the Giu-marras' use of undocumented Mexican workers as strikebreak-ers. Since the ending of the Bracero Program in 1965, agribusi-ness had employed more and more illegal Mexican workers, expanding their profit margin. The media used the popular term *wetbacks* to describe the millions of border crossers who entered the United States without proper documents. Most of those who came for agricultural work crossed the dry desert into California for the spring and summer harvests. But an increasing number were not coming for agricultural jobs: they sought to work in light industry, construction, and service jobs in southern California and the major cities of Texas. In 1968, because of increased protests by organized labor about this threat to U.S. employment, Congress revised the immi-gration laws and established a quota of 120,000 on immigra-tion from Western Hemisphere nations. Mexico's portion of that quota was 20,000 a year.

Despite the new regulations and restrictions, illegal Mexican immigrants continued to head north. To combat the seemingly limitless supply of Mexican strikebreakers, César ordered that UFW members report to the border patrol those ranches that were employing illegal workers. Chávez was convinced that the Immigration and Naturalization Service (INS) was not very diligent in enforcing the regulations so he began pressuring the federal government. When Attorney General Ramsey Clark, in charge of the INS and the border patrol, gave a speech in San Francisco on 30 May, hundreds of UFW pickets greeted him and protested the lack of enforcement of the immigration laws. Six days later, Clark issued orders to toughen the en-forcement procedures. In addition to lobbying the federal agencies, Chávez sent his cousin Manuel to the California border to set up a medical clinic to serve as an organizing center for illegals. The Mexican government had given permission for the UFW to establish the clinic in Mexicali, hoping that Mexican workers using the clinic could be informed of the strike and encouraged to avoid working at the struck ranches.

1968: VIOLENCE AND CHANGE

The year 1968 was a violent one in U.S. history. Americans were frustrated over the lack of progress in both the war in Vietnam and in civil rights. During the first half of the year, 221 student protests exploded, involving more than 40,000 students at 101 campuses across the United States. Maoist and Leninist ideologies influenced many student and radical groups. Organizations like the Black Panthers and the Black Muslims were talking about violent revolution. Moreover, with the growing reports of U.S. deaths and casualties coming from the war in Vietnam, the public was increasingly distrustful of government claims of impending victory. The 1968 Tet offensive in Vietnam had made a mockery of the administration's credibility. Soon after the Tet disaster, President Johnson announced that he would not seek reelection. Almost every night, television news showed the fighting in Vietnam, the police beating antiwar demonstrators, or black youths rampaging in a burning ghetto. People were beginning to be inured to violence. It was increasingly seen as an effetive way to solve domestic and foreign problems.

On 4 April the nation and the world were shocked by the assassination of Dr. Martin Luther King Jr. in Memphis, Tennessee. Soon afterward, riots broke out in Detroit, Cincinnati, Minneapolis, and Washington, D.C. Two months later, on 5 June, another tragedy stunned the nation. Robert Kennedy, brother of the already assassinated JFK, was killed in Los Angeles following his victory in the Democratic primary in California. In August, young people expressed their disapproval of the old-guard politicians by staging protest riots in Chicago during the Democratic convention. The protesters,

led by Jerry Rubin and Abbie Hoffman, were convinced that
the establishment leaders of the Democratic Party represented
a "politics of death."

In New Mexico, violent events involving the Hispano struggle to regain their ancestral lands continued to be prominent
in the news. In January, Reies Tijerina, the fiery land-grant
leader, was released on bond pending his trial for an armed
raid on a courthouse. The previous June, twenty armed members of his Alianza movement had entered the county courthouse in Tierra Amarilla and attempted to carry out a citizens'
arrest of the district attorney, charging that he had violated
their civil rights during a demonstration in the town of Coy-
ote, New Mexico. During the courthouse raid, gunfire broke
out and the Alianza members shot and wounded a state pa-
trolman and an undersheriff. In response to the shootout, the
state government mounted a massive manhunt for Tijerina
and the Alianza members who had been at Tierra Amarilla.
The governor called out a battalion of the National Guard to
join the New Mexico Mounted Patrol, the forest service, and
local Indian deputies. For forty-eight hours, the national guard
held sixty Alianza family members—old men, women, and
children—in a sheep-pen, hoping to lure the fugitives out of
the mountains. The local media called the shootout the beginning of a revolution by "Castro-like terrorists" and the
state called in the FBI. After several weeks of a massive search,
Tijerina and the fugitive members of the Alianza surrendered.
They were charged with twenty-nine counts of kidnapping
and attempted murder. Tijerina was arraigned in court and he
decided to act as his own attorney. In December he was acquitted of the most serious charges.

By 1968, Tierra Amarilla had become a rallying point for
Chicanos throughout the Southwest. A message of support
and solidarity came from Corky Gonzales and his Denver
Crusade for Justice. The Mexican-American Political Associa-
tion (MAPA), a liberal organization in California led by Bert
Corona, announced their support for the Alianza cause. Soon

after the courthouse raid, César Chávez, who was in New Mexico to give a fund-raising address, attended a meeting of Alianza members. He publicly embraced Tijerina and told the cheering audience that he would have been a member of their organization if he had lived in New Mexico. He could identify with their cause "because the issue of the land is crucial to rural Mexicanos and reflects the cruel injustices to which they have been subjected."

This endorsement did not appear to César as contradictory to his own oft-expressed belief in nonviolence. Tijerina did not publicly condone violence, but he recognized that its occurrence was part of the frustration that his followers felt over the land issue. Although Tijerina was acquitted of the charges connected with the courthouse raid, the U.S. Supreme Court rejected an appeal on an earlier conviction and in 1970 Tijerina was sent to prison for two years. His imprisonment destroyed the Alianza movement.

CÉSAR'S TWENTY-FIVE DAY FAST

In this atmosphere of national violence, it was hard to keep the strike against Giumarra from escalating. As usual there had been violent incidents on the picket line. A union member had been run over by a truck and César had to confiscate weapons from picketers who threatened revenge. Several packing sheds had been burned down. Increasingly, among union members, there was talk about retaliation. César felt that violence could end only in destruction of the strike. Once the UFW was associated with violence, it would lose its public support: it was essential that the strikers maintain their discipline. César hit upon a way of demonstrating his commitment to the principle of nonviolence—a fast. "I thought that I had to bring the Movement to a halt, do something that would force them and me to deal with the whole question of violence and ourselves. We had to stop long enough to take account of what we were doing."

In characteristic fashion, he began the fast without telling anyone. He did not know how long it was going to last. On the fourth day, he decided to hold a meeting of the strikers to announce his commitment. "I told them I thought they were discouraged, because they were talking about short cuts, about violence. They were getting so mad with the growers, they couldn't be effective anymore."

He told them that he was going to fast until the members "made up their minds that they were not going to be committing violence" or until they ignored him completely. He decided to conduct the fast at the Forty Acres rather than at home so as not to burden Helen and his family with public attention. At first, his family and friends did not share his commitment for the fast. Helen argued vehemently against it, calling him "ridiculous" and "crazy." Several of the union staff opposed the fast because of ongoing contract negotiations. They proposed a hunger strike, but César opposed any counterfast by union members. The religious implications of this fast antagonized some of the union's leadership and supporters. Antonio Orendain, the secretary-treasurer, for example, strongly opposed any use of religion in union activities. Student liberals and activist volunteers who supported the union also opposed the fast because they saw in it an embarrassing religious display that indirectly supported the hierarchy of the Roman Catholic Church.

After meeting with the membership, Chávez walked to Forty Acres. In a storage room of the service station, he set up a monastic cell, with a small cot and a few religious articles. Soon hundreds of farm-worker families began appearing at the Forty Acres to show their support for Chávez and to attend the daily mass with him. A huge tent-city, with thousands of farm workers, sprang up surrounding the gas station. There was a tremendous outpouring of emotion during the masses. Daily, hundreds stood in line to meet and talk to Chávez. LeRoy Chatfield, who was in charge of the logistics of the fast, said: "César would talk about the workers' home area, he would ask about the conditions there, and then he'd suggest they should try to help themselves, to help form a coordinated effort among the workers, and they would agree." The Mexican and Filipino workers could identify with this leader who wanted to share in their suffering. The fast became an important means of unifying farm workers and educating them about the importance of the strike and boycott.

On the twelfth day of the fast, César had to appear before a judge in Bakersfield to answer a contempt-of-court charge in relation to a court order that the Giumarras had gotten setting restrictions on picketing. When word got out that César needed support, thousands of farm workers appeared and filled the courthouse beyond its capacity, overflowing outside where they sang and prayed on their knees. Most of the time they were completely silent, giving mute testimony to their support for the union's cause. Chávez appeared weak and haggard, barely able to stand. For two successive days, the judge continued the case rather than have to decide against Chávez and eject the farm workers. The media coverage of the event was invaluable in publicizing the boycott and the tactics of the growers.

The national media helped to make César's 1968 fast a major event. As it went into its twentieth day, letters of support came from congressmen, senators, and union and religious leaders. Dr. Martin Luther King Jr.—who was to be assassinated a month later—sent a telegram of support. Robert Kennedy, who had not at that time yet decided to run for the presidency, also sent a telegram, expressing concern for César's health. Chávez would not let a doctor examine him because he felt that "without the element of risk, I would be hypocritical. The whole essence of penance . . . would be taken away."

When Chávez decided to end his fast, on the twenty-fifth day, he asked Robert Kennedy to attend. Their relationship went back to 1959 when, as director of the California CSO, César had met with him to coordinate Democratic voter registration in East Los Angeles. Kennedy conducted the 1966 Senate subcommittee hearings on agricultural labor in De-

Helen Chávez, Robert Kennedy, and Juana Chávez with César Chávez as he breaks his 1968 fast.

lano and had openly expressed his support for the UFW strike and boycott. On 11 March, they held a mass at a county park with more than four thousand farm workers in attendance along with the national media. The mass was said on the back of a flatbed truck. César, too weak to stand, unable to speak, nevertheless had his say: Jim Drake read a message César had written earlier. It was a powerful expression of his spiritual commitment:

> Our struggle is not easy. Those who oppose our cause are rich and powerful, and they have many allies in high places. We are poor. Our allies are few. But we have something the rich do not own. We have our own bodies and spirits and the justice of our cause as our weapons.
>
> When we are really honest with ourselves, we must admit that our lives are all that really belong to us. So it is how we use our lives that determines what kind of men we are. It is my deepest belief that only by giving of our lives do we find life.
>
> I am convinced that the truest act of courage, the strongest act of manliness, is to sacrifice ourselves for others in a totally non-

violent struggle for justice. To be a man is to suffer for others. God help us to be men!

1968–1969: TRAGEDY AND SICKNESS

Soon after the end of the fast, Robert Kennedy announced his intention to run for the Democratic nomination and he asked César to be one of his delegates to the Democratic convention. The union voted affirmatively. Kennedy needed the Mexican-American vote in California to win that state's crucial primary, and having Chávez as a delegate was very helpful. For the next few months, César devoted the energies of the union to a voter-registration drive for Kennedy's campaign. Chávez consulted with Kennedy by phone frequently. Besides embarking on a grueling speaking tour of California to promote the boycott, César organized a drive to register Chicano voters for the 1968 primary election.

The results that summer were tremendously gratifying. Some precincts in East Los Angeles had, for the first time in their history, a 100 percent voter turnout. Almost all voted for Kennedy. According to Bert Corona, state chairman of MAPA at the time, the UFW's mobilization of the Chicano vote in 1968 was a turning point in Chicano politics. It proved to everyone the potential political power in the barrios. After 1968, the base was laid for the election of other Mexican-American office-holders. But tragedy marred the victory. The night of the primary celebration in the Biltmore Hotel in Los Angeles, Sirhan Sirhan shot and killed Robert Kennedy. The nation was devastated. The poor and especially the farm workers had lost a powerful friend and it seemed to be the final blow to the youthful idealism of the 1960s.

After the Kennedy tragedy, health problems incapacitated César for months. In early September 1968 he began suffering severe back pains and was hospitalized for twenty days, but the doctors could not diagnose the cause. He also began losing weight. César thought that he might have cancer. He continued conducting union business from his bed. César had suffered about five months of continual misery when Dr. Janet Travell, who had been President Kennedy's personal physician, visited César at the insistence of Marion Moses, the UFW nurse. Dr. Travell immediately identified the source of the problem: one of César's legs was longer than the other and his spine was being pinched. A few days after being treated, César was able get out of bed and his health gradually improved.

During the winter of 1968 and the spring of 1969, the boycott against table grapes continued. Even though César was immobilized in Delano, he conducted the union business until late at night from his bed. Meanwhile, a Chicano student movement was beginning to take shape, inspired by the organizational successes of the farm workers. In March 1969, Corky Gonzales sponsored a Chicano Youth Liberation Conference in Denver which more than two thousand students attended. At the conference, the students drafted "El Plan Espiritual del Aztlán," a statement calling for self-determination and community control. They proclaimed the creation of a new political movement to energize the growing Chicano populations in the barrios. Within a year, Gonzales and José Angel Gutiérrez, the young political organizer from south Texas, had established La Raza Unida Party, a third-party movement. During subsequent years, this new party challenged the status quo in many small agricultural towns in south Texas and southern Colorado, as well as taking on the Democratic Party in the urban barrios of Los Angeles and San Antonio.

César drew from the growing political consciousness of urban Chicanos by getting volunteers to work in the boycott. In the spring of 1969, to rally support for the strike and boycott, César decided to organize a march through the heart of the Coachella and Imperial Valleys to the United States–Mexico border. One of the primary purposes of the march was to protest grower-use of undocumented immigrants from Mexico as strikebreakers. On 10 May 1969, César began the march in Indio, California, with an outdoor mass celebrated in a labor camp. As in the 1966 march to Sacramento, the Coachella pilgrimage was a tremendous organizing tactic. Hundreds of farm workers and supporters joined in the colorful procession. The Rev. Ralph Abernathy, heir to Dr. Martin Luther King Jr.'s movement, joined the march on the eighth day, pledging the support of the Southern Christian Leadership Conference. Walter Mondale, a liberal senator from Minnesota and future presidential candidate, joined the march along with Hollywood stars and Chicano student activists. The march dramatized the grape strike for scores of Mexican work crews as it passed the fields where they worked. In the evenings, masses, speeches and teatros dramatized the issues.

The march lasted nine days, ending in Calexico, the border town across from Mexicali, Baja California. In Calexico, Chávez gave a speech calling for Mexican workers to join the strike and support the UFW. Before the march reached Calexico, César asked Bert Corona, of MAPA, to go to Mexicali and visit the leaders of the Mexican union to get them to talk to their workers about the strike. Corona gave public service announcements and interviews on radio and television to tell the Mexicans about which ranches were on strike and to explain the issues. Corona's work in Mexico exemplified the international approach that César had been following to stem the tide of strikebreakers.

EL MOVIMIENTO AND THE CHURCH

Chávez relied a great deal on volunteer priests and ministers who flocked to Delano by the score during the late 1960s. He received economic and political support for the union from the Catholic Bishops of California and the California Migrant Ministry. Across the nation, churches, priests, and ministers sympathetic to the farm workers' movement were important in recruiting thousands of volunteers to work on the grape boycott. The prominent role that Roman Catholic priests played in the UFW struggles helped raise expectations of church commitment to issues of social justice, but these hopes were not fulfilled by the church's leadership.

Within urban barrios, Roman Catholic Church support for a more progressive policy to deal with urban problems was not apparent. There were very few Spanish-speaking priests and almost no Spanish-speaking bishops in the church's hierarchy. To protest the neglect of urban issues, Ricardo Cruz in 1969 in Los Angeles organized a group of Mexican Americans. They called themselves Católicos Por La Raza. On Christmas Eve, members of Por La Raza demonstrated their anger over the hierarchy's lack of concern for social justice by picketing the Christmas mass being celebrated at the newly built, opulent St. Basil's Cathedral. Entering the church during the service, they were confronted by club-wielding ushers and a melee broke out, disrupting the mass. National publicity spawned by this incident sensitized some Roman Catholics to Chicano issues. Within a decade, there were significant changes: the appointment of several Spanish-speaking bishops, the recruitment of Latino priests, and the establishment of special programs for Mexican Americans.

VICTORY IN DELANO

By 1969, Chávez decided to expand the boycott to apply to all California table-grape growers, primarily because Giumarra had gotten other Delano growers to supply him with their labels so as to avoid the UFW boycott. Throughout the United States, volunteers began picketing supermarkets that sold grapes. This was a secondary boycott, illegal under the provision of the National Labor Relations Act but entirely legal for the UFW, since farm workers were specifically excluded from coverage in this legislation. Gradually, it became a national moral issue not to eat grapes. Shipments of California table grapes practically stopped to the cities of Boston, New York, Philadelphia, Chicago, Detroit, Montreal, and Toronto. As grape sales fell, millions of pounds of grapes rotted in storage sheds.

In reaction to the boycott, the growers filed a lawsuit charging that they had lost more than $25 million. In desperation they turned to the Teamsters and held meetings to try to work out a contract that would bring peace to the fields. But the Teamsters were leery of entering the fields again, given their experience in the Perelli-Minetti dispute (as recounted above, they were invited in by the growers and kicked out when the pressure became too great). An agreement with the Teamsters fell through after an appeal for an endorsement by Governor Ronald Reagan failed to materialize.

Governor Reagan was sympathetic to the growers. He even appeared on television to urge people to help the farmers and ignore the boycott. And on the national level, the California grape growers had a powerful lobbyist in President Richard Nixon, a former governor of California, who ordered the Defense Department to increase its purchase of table grapes. By the end of 1969, the Department of Defense was buying six times the volume of grapes it had purchased in 1967. Some 2.4 million pounds were shipped to troops in Vietnam. Altogether, the government purchased 9.69 million pounds of grapes that year.

Despite these influential endorsements, boycott pressures began to be unbearable. Gradually, during the late spring of 1969, influential growers in the Coachella Valley went to the negotiating table and signed contracts with the UFW. These growers, Lionel Steinberg and Hollis Roberts, then worked to get other growers to agree to contract negotiations. Soon, UFW grapes, packed in boxes labeled with the union's red and black eagle, were appearing in supermarkets and selling at higher prices than scab grapes. Growers in the Coachella and Bakersfield areas became convinced that it made economic sense to sign union contracts.

By June 1970, the majority of table-grape growers still resisting unionization were in the Delano area. Chávez got Hollis Roberts, the Delano grower who had already signed with the UFW, to use his influence with the other growers. In addition, a committee of bishops from the National Conference of

Catholic Bishops had agreed to act as intermediaries in the dispute. The five-man bishops' committee brought the two sides together to settle the four-year grape strike. The results were dramatic. On 16 July, Chávez called an emergency meeting. After a mass, César read a message he had received from Bishop Joseph Donnelly: "The table grape growers listed below have authorized Philip J. Feick, Jr., Western Employers Council, Bakersfield, California, to negotiate on their behalf with the United Farm Workers Organizing Committee for purposes of effecting a labor agreement between the parties."

Twenty-three companies, including Giumarra, had agreed to begin negotiations to recognize the UFW. The talks were scheduled to commence the next day. For two days, the growers met with the UFW representatives in a motel room in Bakersfield. Progress was made, but the discussions came to a halt when the growers refused to travel to the union's headquarters at Forty Acres to sign the contracts. Simultaneously, they hardened their position on several issues and finally walked out of the meeting.

The day after the talks collapsed, César got a phone call from someone in Salinas telling him that the Teamsters were signing up workers in the lettuce fields and promising to sign contracts with the lettuce growers. Their actions were in violation of the jurisdictional agreement that had been reached several years earlier. César decided to meet the challenge vigorously. On July 25, he drove to Salinas and held a press conference, announcing that the UFW demanded the growers immediately recognize the UFW and enter into negotiations. In strategy sessions with local workers, he planned a march through the Salinas Valley to rally support.

When he returned to Delano late Saturday night, Chávez learned that Giumarra wanted immediately to resume the negotiations. At about 2 A.M. John Giumarra met César in Room 44 of the Stardust Motel in Delano and reopened negotiations. By 9 A.M. Sunday they had reached an agreement and Giumarra got all the growers in Delano to meet with the

UFW that afternoon to negotiate a final contract. By Monday night, all major points had been settled and plans were made to finalize the agreement.

On 29 July 1970, twenty-nine grape growers assembled in Reuther Hall at Forty Acres, near Delano, to sign union contracts with the UFW. Because of the packed throng, the growers had to enter the hall through a back door and sit in the few empty seats at the front of the auditorium, facing the farm workers they had been battling for five years. The tension in the room was palpable—relieved only briefly by a cheery John Giumarra who gave a brief speech about unity and peace. César was wearing a Filipino shirt and looked tired from the marathon bargaining sessions that he had been through in recent weeks. One by one the growers signed their contracts, giving farm workers a wage of $1.80 per hour and contributing 10 cents per hour to the Robert Kennedy Health and Welfare Fund; another 2 cents per hour to UFW service centers. The contracts all had provisions for a hiring hall and controls over pesticide usage. As each grower signed, the assembly of farm workers cheered and sang, beginning a celebration that continued all that historic day.

Chávez's response to the dramatic victory was typically philosophical. He spoke of the sacrifices that the workers had made: "Ninety five percent of the strikers lost their homes and their cars. But I think that in losing those worldly possessions they found themselves, and they found that only through dedication, through serving mankind, and, in this case, serving the poor, and those who were struggling for justice, only in that way could they really find themselves."

The victory in Delano now meant that 85 percent of all table-grape growers in California were under a union contract. This sweeping victory was without precedent in the history of U.S. agriculture. Never before had an agricultural workers' union managed such a success.

For Chávez, the celebration was short-lived. He had learned

a few days before the triumphant signing ceremony that the Teamsters had signed several dozens of contracts with vegetable growers in the Salinas Valley. The Teamsters clearly, once again, were trying to take away UFW contracts. This new threat was one of the greatest to the existence of the union.

CHAPTER 6

César Chávez and American Liberals

Our opponents must understand that it is not just a union we have built. Unions, like other institutions, come and go. But . . . our union has been on the cutting edge of a people's course and you cannot do away with an entire people.

CÉSAR CHÁVEZ

EVERYTHING in the United States seemed to be transforming when César Chávez founded his association to help farm workers. The country was undergoing radical political and cultural change. The central tenets of American liberalism, that philosophy identified with the New Deal, seemed under siege. During this turbulent period, the old-style liberals—people such as Arthur M. Schlesinger Jr.—thought that "the basic task [was] to control and humanize the forces of change in order to prevent them from tearing our society apart."

The same year that Chávez began the grape strike (1965), the black movement had begun to change from a focus on nonviolent struggle for civil rights to an emphasis on violent racial confrontation and separatism. In addition, increasing U.S. involvement in Vietnam soon exploded into a decade of frustration and civil disorder. The cultural radicals, most dramatically embodied in the hippie movement, were emphasizing a new lifestyle of free love, drugs, and an overthrow of middle-class values. Lyndon Johnson was on the verge of initiating his Great Society and the welfare state. Most Americans, without knowing it, were about to embark on the construction of postmodern America: a world of ambiguity, economic despair, political frustration, and self-doubt. Perhaps most importantly, the United States and most of the rest of the world was becoming engaged in a struggle with youth—a world-wide movement of young people that would question family values, political attitudes, liberalism, capitalist institutions, and democratic authority. The United States, during the 1960s, was a society searching for its soul, a nation questioning its own identity, and a culture at war with itself.

This self-doubt was especially frustrating for the American liberal intelligentsia. U.S. New Deal–type liberalism rested on the central values under direct assault: individualism, the work ethic, the family, political pluralism, democratic politics, patriotism. All of U.S. civic culture, in fact, was being threatened, especially the central notions of freedom, equality, constitutionalism, federalism, and social and class mobility.

Many leftist intellectuals wanted to weave a new sociopolitical cloth. As radical theorist Stanley Aronowitz wrote of New Left intellectuals: "Writers like [William Appleman] Williams . . . Gabriel Kolko and [James] Weinstein . . . shaped a new vision of the 20th century of American corporate liberalism which became probably the most influential doctrine of American historiography in the 1960s." This vision of the past argued that the United States in the twentieth century had been dominated by multinational corporations and that New Deal liberalism was fundamentally a rationale to continue with the hegemony of American capitalist imperialism. The *New Left Review* and *Studies on The Left* became major theoretical journals of the new "liberal" Left, which was led by intellectuals such as Weinstein, Aronowitz, Tom Hayden, Eugene Genovese, Staughton Lynd, C. Wright Mills, and others. These journals, together with leftist intellectuals and radical social movements headed by ethnic and racial groups, threatened the ideological hegemony of the old-style, New Deal liberal intellegentsia.

Cultural and political radicals within the youth movement urged the adoption of new heroes—heroes threatening to tear down the system that liberals sought to preserve. Herbert Marcuse, Che Guevara, Lenin, Trotsky, Mao, Malcolm X, Za-

pata, Villa. After John F. Kennedy's death, the liberal establishment sought other heroes to exemplify the Jeffersonian
ideals being attacked by the growing cultural and political
revolution. Peter Clecak, a liberal intellectual who turned conservative, wrote: "The dreams of the New Frontier and the
Great Society dissolved into the nightmare of Vietnam, intensified racism, urban violence, and student unrest. Expectations, heightened in part by the growth and dissemination of
social commentary, were deflated, and faith in the value of criticism as a prelude to remedial action correspondingly waned."
César Chávez and the United Farm Workers provided a fresh
vision for a liberal community that was increasingly demor-
alized.

THE AIM OF LIFE IS . . . COOPERATION

Throughout the turbulent 1960s, César Chávez began to be
identified by liberals as a symbol of the older values—this in a
world where people were wondering whether order still ex-
isted. César Chávez placed change and continuity into perspective in this way:

> As for the nation as a whole, it doesn't matter to me how our
> government is structured or what type of political party one may
> have. The real change comes about when men really want it. In a
> small way, we try to change ourselves and we try to change those
> with whom we come into contact. You can't organize the masses
> unless you organize individuals. I like to think of our groups as a
> "doer" type union. We place a great deal of emphasis on doing
> things and very little on theorizing or writing about them. . . . We
> must acquaint people with peace—not because capitalism is bet-
> ter or communism is better, but because, as men we are better. . . .
> We need a cultural revolution. And we need a cultural revolution
> among ourselves not only in art but also in the realm of the spirit.
> As poor people and immigrants, all of us [Americans and Mexi-
> cans] have brought to this country some very important things of
> the spirit. . . . We must never forget that the human element is the
> most important thing we have—if we get away from this, we are
> certain to fail.

Chávez wanted change, but with continuity; a cultural revolution, without political revolution; an emphasis on a renewal of national, individual, and human spirit. Liberal intellectuals, engulfed in a sea of radicalism, gravitated toward him.

Chávez was engaged in a political and social revolution. The rest of the country, especially other ethnic minorities, Anglo-American students, and women, were also involved in this revolution. However, many ethnics sought a violent revolution, the politics of exclusion, and a society of multiculturalism. They sought, as historian Daniel Boorstein often stated, the balkanization and fragmentation of the United States. Most of the youths, women, and ethnics who were engaged in a utopian revolt during the 1960s believed that political equality was the aim of life, sexual love the basis of happiness, and free choice the basis of politics. This philosophy turned the liberal outlook upside down. From Jefferson on, liberals had argued that happiness was the aim of life, that virtue was the basis of happiness, and that utility was the main criterion of virtue. Interestingly, Chávez's philosophy closely paralleled these Jeffersonian ideas.

THE LAST JEFFERSONIAN

For Chávez, cooperation was the aim of life; common respect was the basis of cooperation and happiness; and spirituality and humanism were the criteria of respect. As Chávez clearly stated, "I think that our philosophy of cooperation with all groups has helped us a great deal. Our people have developed the ability to respect every one with whom they came into contact." Yet, like Jefferson's, Chávez's ideas contained paradoxes: he sought cooperation, but understood the need for power; he respected individualism, but understood that the movement must be built on the collective; he sought a change of society, but understood that it must begin with each person's humanity. Chávez shunned philosophy and theory because he knew that in the United States change came from doing. As Chávez wrote: "We place a great deal of emphasis on doing things and very little on theorizing or writing about them. . . . It is necessary to build a power base, but it must be built on people, not money." If workers are going to do anything, he said, "they need their own power." Chávez almost instinctively knew that power lay in changing *people*; not by theorizing but by doing. Not through violence but through nonviolence.

Chávez also understood that national unity was more powerful politically than ethnic separatism. Consequently, he argued that poor people and immigrants "all . . . have brought to this country some very important things of the spirit. But too often, they are choked; they are not allowed to flourish in our society. People are not going to turn back now. The poor are on the march: black, brown, red, everyone, whites included." Chávez believed in what philosopher Adrienne Koch has said Jefferson believed in: "the fresh contacts with the commanding personalities and events of these days, and for the fullest expression of government through consent, through reason, through energetic and progressive change." Both the philosophy of Jefferson and the image of Chávez were anomalies in the late 1960s world of militancy, violence, power, exclusion, hatred, and racism. As a result, old-style liberals turned to Chávez as the last Jeffersonian and the central hope of a new American revolution.

*   *   *   *   *

Four key liberal intellectuals illustrate the popular cultural view of Americans toward César Chávez. These four writers interpreted the public persona of Chávez until it became both a vital window to the liberal soul and a mirror that reflected into the future.

MATTHIESSEN: CHÁVEZ AND THE AMERICAN REVOLUTION

In the late 1960s, Peter Matthiessen, a nature/travel writer and investigative novelist under contract with Random House, went to investigate and write about the "species mexicana" in the habitat of the Southwest. But this was more than one of Matthiessen's quests to uncover the essence of nature: it was an attempt to find the "lost soul" of American society. He was in pursuit of what Eldridge Cleaver had suggested was America's "soul on ice."

Matthiessen, in almost an archaeological fashion, approached Delano, California, the center of farm-worker activities, which he quickly pointed out to his American audience was pronounced *De-lay-no.* Matthiessen was clearly aware that most Americans, especially Easterners, had not heard much about Mexican Americans (and even less of their militant offsprings who were asserting a new political awareness under the theme of Chicanismo) except as poor forgotten farm workers, maids, or gardeners.

As Matthiessen was beginning his book, another liberal, Stan Steiner, was writing another book on the rising Chicano movement in the Southwest. And here it is worth breaking away for a moment from Matthiessen to quote what was then a newly established liberal-radical publication, the *New York Review of Books.* It set the tone for Matthiessen, Steiner, and other American liberals. Edgar Friedenberg wrote in the midst of the 1960s radicalism,

> the [Mexican-American farmer workers are] the only people I had seen in months who seemed positively happy and free from self-pity. In their response to me, they have been friendlier and more open, by far, than most of the people I meet, though my speech and manner must have struck them as very unlike their own. I wondered why they had trusted me. I realized that, of course, they hadn't. It was themselves they had trusted. Such people do not fear strangers. Whether he wins La Huelga or not, this Cesar Chavez has done, or rather, has taught his people to do for themselves [what the rest of us still cannot do]. Nothing I know of in the history of labor in American shows as much creativity . . . as much respect for what people, however poor, might make of their own lives once they understood the dynamics of their society.

Here Friedenberg was establishing the new liberal textual representation of Chávez and the farm workers that expressed the perspective of other intellectuals. Mexican Americans, specifically the farm workers and César Chávez, were existentially authentic, primarily because of their labor, their relationship to the land, their respect for their humanity, and their love of community. The Mexican farm worker was closer to the Jeffersonian ideal of the true "common man." As farm workers, they were God's chosen children, threatened by an industrial society. For Friedenberg, Matthiessen, and other liberal thinkers, Chávez and his agricultural strikers were remade as the lost heirs of Jefferson and the last hope of America in the turbulent 1960s.

Matthiessen sensed a "natural" authenticity of Mexican farm workers and the sincerity and humanity of their culture. He wrote: "Chávez is a plain spoken man who does not waste his own time or his listener's with false humility, yet he is uncomfortable when the necessity arises to speak about himself, and may even emit a gentle groan." For the American intellectual, such as Matthiessen, Chávez represented the antithesis of the Ugly American. Even the union newspaper *El Malcriado*, Matthiessen pointed out, was written in a tone of earthy sophistication. It is, he wrote, not "propagandistic" or "shrill." It was "slanted but not irresponsible, and well-edited."

Matthiessen, as well as other liberals, was also attracted by the commonsense clarity and magnitude of the Mexican-American farm workers' struggle against rich and powerful agribusiness. Ironically, the innocent, clearly agrarian, and virtuous perception at the heart of the farm workers' movement has always been the U.S. nation's historical image of itself. As a result, the farm workers were philosophically "discovered" by U.S. liberal intellectuals and politicians, such as Robert Kennedy, as being real Jeffersonian Americans. Matthiessen fashioned this image of the farm workers and César Chávez from his observer-participatory analysis in 1968.

But Matthiessen saw in the Chávez struggle something more. He wrote: "I feel that the farm workers' plight is [also] related to all of America's most serious affiliations: racism, poverty, environment pollution, and urban crowding and decay—all of these compounded by the waste of [the Vietnam] war." In the farm workers, Matthiessen had discovered a classic ethnographic representative model of people who not only could be studied, but who could be the "other" that could save the soul and environment of America. The farm workers represented a moral and ecological alternative to a decaying world. Using his naturalist background, he continued: "In a damaged human habitat, all problems merge. For example, noise, crowding, and smog poisoning are notorious causes of human irritability; that crowded ghettos explode first in the worst smog areas of America is no coincidence at all." From this perspective, Chávez and his farm workers were not only a metaphor for the soul of the United States; they were also a model by which the specific problems of the 1960s and the general problems of modernity could be studied and possibly eliminated. These interpretations reflected the fears and hopes of the liberal intelligencia more than the day-to-day realities of Chávez's struggle which in their writings appeared to be more of an ideological struggle than a trade union fight. But it was true that there was an element of undefinable spirituality about La Causa. Perhaps it was this element that attracted liberal thinkers to Chávez.

For Matthiessen, the agricultural land issue between farm worker and farm owner that Chávez was trying to confront had a larger implication. It was analogous to the ecological problem of balance in human and animal society. For example, in animal society, rats overpopulate and pollute their environment. This in turn led to "increased incidence of homosexuality, gang rape, killing, and consumption by the mothers of their young." The ecological conditions caused by an unbalanced rat population were analogous to the actions of agribusiness: agribusiness upset a natural balance. For Matthiessen, Chávez was a potential center of the ecological movement—although, in the 1960s, the union movement was ostensibly about wages, conditions, racism, and redressing the 1935 National Labor Relations Act (the Wagner Act). As Chávez succinctly put it: the movement was basically one for people *buscando trabajo* (looking for work).

Matthiessen saw Chávez as almost the last Jeffersonian fighting for a "new/old ethic" in a world where cultural radicals were seeking to destroy middle-class America. The New Left sought to change the politics of capitalism; the ethnics wanted a separation from the unity of *E Pluribus Unum;* and the women's movement strove to redefine the "biological and cultural" definitions of gender. Matthiessen aptly entitled his text, *César Chávez and the New American Revolution.* His title suggested, Matthiessen stated, that

> before this century is done, there will be an evolution in our values and the values of human society, not because man has become more civilized, but because, on a blighted earth, he will have no choice. This evolution—actually a revolution where violence will depend on the violence with which it is met—must aim at an order of things that treats man and his habitat with respect; the new order, grounded in human ecology, will have humanity as its purpose and the economy as its tool. . . . [The hope] of orderly change depends on men like César Chávez, who, of all leaders now in sight, best represents the rising generations.

For Matthiessen and many liberals Chávez not only represented hope, but a faith in the notions of innocence, responsibility, justice, freedom of the individual, and attachment to community power. Chávez, Matthiessen wrote, is "an idealist unhampered by Ideology, an activist with a near-mystic vision, a militant with a dedication to nonviolence, and he stands free of the political machinery that the election year 1968 [police violence in Chicago against young people at the Democratic convention] made not only disreputable, but irrelevant." Chávez represented in Matthiessen's mind (and the minds of many of his nonethnic supporters) a public leader who could organize a "rainbow coalition" without ideology or discrimination, because Chávez sought diversity within unity. This multi-ethnicity was evident in the makeup of his staff. He espe-

cially sought nonideological personnel who were basically pragmatic; for example, LeRoy Chatfield, a key assistant; Jim
Drake, administrative assistant; staff lawyers Jerome Cohen
and David Averbuck; David Fishlow, an early editor of *El
Malcriado,* as well as the top Mexican-American and Filipino
staff, Dolores Huerta, Manuel and Richard Chávez, Philip
Vera Cruz, Larry Itliong, and Gil Padilla. This diverse but
united leadership for a New American Revolution reflected
what Matthiessen wanted to introduce to all Americans.

Chávez and his movement in the 1960s served as a prism.
One saw in him what one wanted to see. For religious clergy,
it was a Christian movement; for youth, it was a communal-
mystical movement; for political radicals, it was a labor-class
struggle; for liberal intellectuals and politicians, it was a movement of hope and the American essence; and for others, Chávez
was another Gandhi.

Chávez thrived in these roles, although fundamentally he
believed he was just a man of truth. Chávez's office mirrored
his multifaceted public image. The walls displayed the variety
of the imposed perceptions: photographs of Robert and John
F. Kennedy, of Gandhi and Zapata, an image of the Virgin de
Guadalupe; and of course the thunderbird union flag, along
with U.S. and Mexican flags. Running like a thread through
these diverse perceptions was a common element: his supporters framed Chávez as a person one could trust, a man with
strong personal and family values, who loved his country and
the ideals of love of equality, freedom, and justice. Here was a
man of dignity who respected differences, who stood for community and work, who led a simple life, who loved God, and
who, above all, fought against any oppression by the rich.
Only the extreme Republican right wing saw him as part of
a Communist plot. In the world of the sixties, when many traditional values were being questioned, Chávez appealed to a
majority of Americans. He was a carrier of universality and
continuity rather than of relativism and radical change. For
Americans, to support Chávez was also to support themselves

against the "politics of change" and the "crises of culture."
Chávez's cry of *Ya basta!* (enough) was also, it seemed, the cry
of his diverse supporters.

Chávez, without much formal education and with manner-
isms that often appeared peasantlike, was seen by many as a
simple, trustworthy individual—honest, sincere, and dedicated
to a struggle for *Los de abajo*—(the oppressed). Describing
Chávez's physical appearance, Matthiessen wrote of him: "He
was wearing his invariable costume plaid shirt, work pants,
dark suede shoes—but he was clean and neatly pressed." Americans responded to this representative, innocent vision, especially when Chávez used his favorite proverb: *Hay mas tiempo
que vida* (there is more time than life). He usually added: "We
don't worry about time because time and history are on our
side." Many Americans responded to this figure of innocence
and simplicity, especially in a context in which the growers
were characterized, by Mattiessen and other writers, as rich,
menacing, and ruthless. Americans have often sided with the
Davids against the Goliaths and with the poor against the
rich, and Chávez represented this form of struggle. (It may be
noted, however, that this perspective was not as active in the
views of many Americans about the war in Vietnam.) What
Matthiessen and most Americans saw in Chávez were the
qualities the founding fathers had in 1776: hope, dedication,
perseverance, principles, and chutzpah. Above all, in Chávez
Matthiessen saw America's hope for humanity, faith in God,
and love of basic political virtues. These were at the core of
Chávez and the farm workers' movement. Matthiessen wrote:
"César Chávez shares this astonishing hope of an evolution in
human values, and I do too; it is the only hope we have [in the
sixties]." Matthiessen, thus, saw Chávez as the metaphor of a
man trapped in the fate of postmodern destructive despair,
but who could still cry out, "Wait, have faith. . . . I love you."
For Matthiessen, these words were God's message, through
Chávez, who would lead the New American Revolution.

Matthiessen put it succinctly at the end of his epilogue:

"Chávez's cause had become a holding action for [the societal] change that was inevitable, a clash of citizens versus consumers, quality versus quantity, freedom versus conformism and fear. And sooner or later, the new citizens would win, for the same reason that other Americans [had] won, two centuries ago, because time and history are on their side, and passion." In the world of the sixties, to most Americans change seemed to be not only inevitable, but likely to be catastrophic.

LEVY: CHÁVEZ AS COLLECTIVE SELF

Matthiessen had seen in Chávez the revolution of faith, hope, and trust: another writer, Jacques E. Levy, saw Chávez as the collective self of the farm workers and the American people. In the 1960s, individualism had taken a frontal attack from the New Left and countercultural revolutionaries. These movements had sought to destroy individualism and resurrect the collective. However, Chávez, as perceived by Levy in *Autobiography*, sought to identify and retain the self, although the self as embedded in the collective, the community.

Chávez was opposed to having an intellectual write an "autobiography" of him that would make him into a hero, but he recognized the importance that a narrative of the union could have in showing the spirit of collectivity. Levy worked with the farm workers as he wrote his book and Chávez accepted this textual representation.

Because Levy understood that Chávez did not want an autobiography, he titled his book, *César Chávez: Autobiography of La Causa*. He wrote: "This, then, is not César Chávez's autobiography. It is the story of his life in his own words, but it lacks the key ingredient of an autobiography—the decision of what to include and what to emphasize. [It is an] accurate portrait of a man and a movement engaged in a struggle for social change."

Chávez here only briefly embodies old-style individualism and radical unionism: between 1965 and 1976, Chávez was between the paradoxes and ironies of capitalism and his struggle for societal cooperation based on a deep faith in humanity and justice; and Levy captures this essence of Chávez and the farm workers caught up in a rupture of time. Truth, Levy argued, was the essence of Chávez. Chávez, for Levy, personified truth: not the current political ideologies in the United States but more a moral truth. For Chávez, truth was the ultimate weapon. As he himself stated: "Truth is nonviolence. So everything really comes from truth. Truth is God." Chávez also believed that truth "is on our side, even more than justice, because truth can't be changed. It has a way of manifesting itself. It has to come out, so sooner or later, we'll win."

In Chávez, Levy had confronted the obvious: like the proverbial boy who dared to shout that the emperor had no clothes, César proclaimed that American society had no truth in its core of existence. Levy argued that Chávez and his movement were exposing this "darker" side of America. Many believed that America was based on the continuing universal values of freedom, honesty, respect, justice, fairness, community, and family. But Chávez suggested that the United States was, in fact, a country built on commercialism, capitalism, consumerism, industrialism, advertising, and an overall philosophy of relativism.

In his portrait of Chávez, Levy sought to find the heart of American society, and he found what appeared to be a moralistic truism. When Levy probed, he found that truth in Chávez led to an emphasis on justice, but when this social justice was concretely applied, it led to an ideology of traditional unionism. Nevertheless, liberals between 1965 and through the 1970s were attracted to Chávez because he spoke the truth—about the growers, Vietnam, economic oppression, social injustices, and political oppression. Liberals, as well as radicals, ethnics, clergy, continued to flock to Chávez as long as the thematic emphasis of the farm workers' struggle was just predicated on a broad program of truth, justice, fairness, love, humanity, and hope, and against general oppression and human debasement. This moralism was Chávez's innocent and nonideological side. On this side, Levy saw in Chávez the lost soul of American society. This was especially evident to him when Levy began his book in 1969.

By the time Levy finished *Autobiography* in 1974, he recognized Chávez's need for an ideological program. This was Chávez's other side. Chávez articulated the outlines of this ideology to Levy in 1974:

> Once we have reached our goal [against the growers] and have farm workers protected by contracts, we must continue to keep our members involved. The only way is to continue struggling. It's just like plateaus. We get a union. Then we want to struggle for something else. After contracts, we have to build more clinics and co-ops, and we've got to resolve the whole question of mechanization. Then there is the whole question of political action. We have to participate in the governing of towns and school boards. We have to make our influence felt everywhere and anywhere. Political power alone is not enough. Effective political power is never going to come, particularly to minority groups, unless they have economic power.
>
> I'm not advocating black capitalism or brown capitalism. What I'm suggesting [is] a cooperative movement. Power can come from credit in a capitalistic society, and credit in a society like ours means people. As soon as you're born, you're worth so much— not in money, but in the privilege to get in debt. And I think that's a powerful weapon. If you have a lot of people, then you have a lot of credit. The idea is to organize that power [of credit] and transfer it into something real.

Chávez's ideology, as reflected in this statement, was centered on power, struggle, and progress. However, Chávez admitted that he knew little about economic theory, although he was always clear that power had to be in the hands of the poor and the minorities. He thought that if they could control their economic destiny, as well as their political destiny, they could have power over their lives. Chávez never was quite clear, it seems, on whether he was only talking about wages, a new economic system, or workers' participation in society's structural decisionmaking. He spoke in such generalities that people knew only that he wanted to have the farm workers and the poor have more control over their lives. For Chávez, as he indicated in his comments to "autobiographer" Levy, each person at birth had a potential earning power for his or her lifetime. This was what he meant by "credit": the money and profits were initially in the hands of the individual. What Chávez wanted was for the poor to control their own lifetime earning power—their lifetime "credit." This was control over personal labor and personal surplus value. In many ways, this sounded like community control of neighborhood businesses or the notion of black capitalism, although Chávez did not accept this comparison.

On the other hand, by the "privilege to get in debt" Chávez meant people selling their lifetime's labor to employers without having any option; i.e., having to work for wages. Chávez was never clear philosophically or idealogically about what he wanted. Nevertheless, his passions, his instincts, his desires were correct: he wanted justice for the poor. He knew what he did not want, but he was not sure what he wanted. His problem translates into the classic paradox faced by leftist movements in the United States since the 1930s when many unions rejected Marxism, communism, and socialism.

Chávez said: "I guess I have an ideology, but it probably cannot be described in terms of any political or economic system. But, I think some power has to come to them [farm workers and the poor] so they can manage their lives. I don't care what system it is; it's not going to work if they don't have power." Chávez was unclear about economic theory or what could insure power to the workers since he seemed to reject all *isms*. He was clear on only one thing: he wanted a democratic system: "That's why if we make democracy work, I'm convinced that's by far the best system and it will work if people want it to." However, for Chávez democracy was not just a political system: it was a societal élan vital; a Christian ethos: charity and individual dignity. In general, Chávez advocated a "culture of social justice."

In this, Chávez was closer to theologian Paul Tillich's *New*

Being of love and faith and Reinhold Niebuhr's Christian Realism than to Marx, Castro, Lenin, or the utopian socialists. Chávez himself said: "I was convinced [that my ideology was] . . . very Christian. That's my interpretation. I don't think it was so much political or economic." This Christian democratic vagueness, strong in its appeal, was weak in guiding policy. A collective movement moves on the wheels of ideology, a pulsating vision or a need to implement a philosophical system, but for Chávez the conceptual system for a just society was not carried in the collective consciousness of a movement, but in the consciousness of each individual. The new society for Chávez resided in the heart of every man and woman as each practiced a life of sacrifice and charity. For Chávez, only a union in the pragmatic tradition of Samuel Gompers (the nineteenth-century AFL organizer) could deliver "bread and butter" while giving people the opportunity collectively to sacrifice and commit themselves to a life of charity via union activity. Unfortunately, Chávez was not very clear on the direction that his union or the AFL-CIO should take.

In 1974 (the year before the publication of Levy's book), as the activist period of the Chicano movement was ebbing along with the antiwar movement and other radical causes, Chávez moved from a general vision of "the sacrificing-self" to that of a "unionist-self" from being the young leader of a union in 1965 he had become a leader of an American and Chicano movement; now he reverted to his union role. Levy had insight into Chávez when he wrote in 1974 that "in the future, César Chávez and his followers will repeat the [union] tactics they have used in the past." Levy observed that Chávez was a populist leader who was significant because he showed "the way to meaningful social change by using militant non-violent tactics and organizing people of various backgrounds, political persuasions, and faiths. In an era of great cynicism, La Causa is showing that individuals can make a difference, can help themselves and others, and can keep the principles, although the task is hard and is never-ending."

LONDON AND ANDERSON: CHÁVEZ THE SELFLESS

Joan London and Henry Anderson, the first academics to explore the rise of Chávez and the farm workers' movement, entitled their book *So Shall Ye Reap*, suggesting that agribusiness itself sowed the problems of farm worker oppression. Their harvest—the consequence—was Chávez and his movement. For London and Anderson, Chávez was a man who, rising out of poverty, was psychologically shaped by a personal need to sacrifice. He had a strong pragmatic approach to issues and problems; he was an indirect product of Saul Alinsky's method of organizing, via the tutelage of Fred Ross.

In Chávez's upbringing, according to London and Anderson, there were no traces of ideological dogmatism or demagoguery. But there was a history of reliance on people to organize power and identify issues. As a result, Chávez believed in picketing, boycotting, sit-ins: "appropriate forms of action." He did not believe in intellectual or theoretical approaches and was pragmatic in his approach to organizing.

London and Anderson narratively describe Chávez as just a pragmatic American—an Alinsky-type organizer who was a modest, self-sacrificing man, guided by a populist conscience, and informed by an insider's understanding of the problems of the farm workers. Chávez was not an outside agitator but a hardworking, selfless individual. London and Anderson believed that Chávez was very cognizant of Christian values.

Liberal intellectuals such as London and Anderson, like Mattheissen and Levy, suggest that Chávez was not outside the American tradition. He was a man who, early in life, had felt a basic need to struggle to get ahead and was endowed with not only an independent spirit but "deep convictions about justice." London and Anderson tell of a man who "fundamentally [was] a very good, shrewd, hard-working organizer of unorganized people, equipped with an unusually well-integrated philosophy of how to go about it, and why." In short, they say Chávez had "good American common sense." He worked to organize a union in a traditional American fashion and did not have "selfish ambitions."

Writing in 1970, London and Anderson painted for American readers what they felt was lacking in the world of hippies, New Leftists, feminists, ethnic nationalists, student radicals, Marxist organizers, and antiwar activists: a homegrown American organizer who had the tendencies of a Gandhi but was not necessarily "saintly, heroic" or even "charismatic." Chávez, for London and Anderson, was an American who "deserves to be honored not for [his leadership or charismatic qualities] but for building social structures which will go on fulfilling their functions regardless of the personal qualities of his successors. His basic method, which has amply proved its value to the farm labor movement, is potentially of equal value to many other groups trying to win themselves a better life."

This was the popular view of Chávez: an American organizer who had at heart the interests of everyman. Chávez, in the London and Anderson text, was the selfless guy who lived next door. He emerged, with a Horatio Alger style, to be a leader because he possessed simple American values and the virtue of doing manual work, as well as an intolerance for unfairness. "Americans," London and Anderson wrote, "are sometimes tolerant of unfairness for long periods of time (but not forever). They are capable of selfishness, prejudice, and other human failings." London and Anderson saw Chávez as having the same value system as most Americans—a system that stressed the very qualities called for by the farm-labor movement: freedom of association, self-determination, and fair play. "It is always to the advantage of any social movement if, rather than demanding a whole new set of social values, it asks society simply to live up to those which it already professes," they wrote. Chávez, they said, fitted this mold. This was America, and Americans acted not out of Jeffersonian sentiments (as Matthiessen believed) nor through the collective individualism (Levy) but out of pragmatic, associative impulses.

Americans, for liberals of the London and Anderson type, needed a person—like Chávez—who simply rebelled against "human debasement, and the estrangement of man from his work, from the land [and] from his fellowman." As London and Anderson put it: "As ye sow, so shall ye reap the seeds. The seeds of bondage produced alien strains which choked other plantings in our fields. This bitter harvest will not continue much longer. The tares will be rooted out, and sweeter harvests will begin, because the soil of America is, in the last analysis, congenial to the seeds of the farm labor movement, and uncongenial to injustice." For London and Anderson, Chávez personified the hardworking American man who rises to leadership; who can move and manipulate coalitions and associations to weed out the injustices alien to the United States. There was nothing, they said, heroic or unique about Chávez except that he was American: and Americanism is unique.

MEANWHILE, FOR CHÁVEZ . . .

Regardless of the public perception of César Chávez as a leader of the New American Revolution, a Gandhi, an Alinskian organizer, a metaphor for Jeffersonian morality, or as just a plain American, he was a profound individual because of his personal honesty, truthfulness, and dignity; therefore, he was an enticing image for Americans and they embraced him and his movement. In a world in revolt, the liberal intelligentsia— in search of a hero, of a myth, of a soul—performed the necessary textual transfiguration. Not that Chávez was *not* a strong and charismatic leader and an effective organizer; but the liberals built up a larger-than-life image of him. They needed this image of Chávez during the 1960s radical critique of American culture and society. When the United States encountered the end of the Vietnam War and the end of the 1960s political era, Chávez, who was not an intellectual, a businessman, or a commanding politician, began to diminish in size, appeal, and support. It was time for the Nixon era and

the "era of narcissism." Chávez did not change: conditions
changed.

In the 1970s, the union movement gave Chávez a forum in
which he could use his organizing skills and continue with a
simple but important vision of struggle: workers versus the
corporations. But in a postmodern United States, the frontlines
of the power struggle had moved. Chávez, like Booker T.
Washington at the end of the nineteenth century, no longer
had a viable national vision. Chávez, who had always believed
in the dignity of the common man and emphasized the values
of hope, faith, work, and brotherhood, followed the direction
history and his skills had pushed him toward: the labor union
struggle and the role of a union leader.

The intellectuals' perceptions and writings had shaped Chávez into a people's icon, a leader of the soul of America. But all
their interpretations of his persona were created textual repre-
sentations. For Chávez, life was not intellectually complex. He
did not agonize like Jefferson over industrialization and urban-
ization. He was not rent like Henry Adams over modernity.
Chávez believed in a simple truth. As he said: "Fighting for
social justice, it seems to me, is one of the profoundest ways
in which man can say yes to man's dignity, and that really
means sacrifices."

For Chávez, truth, dignity, and faith were the simple, basic
tenets of his belief system. Ironically, his interpreters established a more complex role for him in the history of the period, reflecting as much their needs as the realities of Chávez
and the farm workers. Chávez had central private beliefs, but
the old-style liberals created his public person. Levy acknowledged the continual shifting of the interpretation of Chávez.
"This, then," he wrote, "is the story of César Chávez and La
Causa—[It is] the truth as perceived by those who lived it
and witnessed it." Little did the liberal intellectuals, and even
Chávez, know that, with the end of militancy, the Cold War,
and communism in the 1980s and 1990s, the truths of Chávez's world would be increasingly perceived as problematic.

CHAPTER 7

Fragile Victories

History will judge societies and governments—and their institutions—not by how big they are or how well they serve the rich and the powerful, but by how effectively they respond to the needs of the poor and the helpless.

CÉSAR CHÁVEZ

A union organizer once compared César Chávez's lifework to that of Sisyphus, the Corinthian king who was condemned by the gods forever to push a huge stone to the top of a hill only to have it roll down again when he neared the top. Indeed, César might have been forgiven if he had considered the history of the UFW during the 1970s and 1980s to have been a form of Greek tragedy. There were tremendous struggles. César and the other UFW organizers, facing tremendous obstacles, from time to time enjoyed temporary victories; always, however, they had to start over again, struggling to build the union. That the struggle continued was mostly due to the strength and perseverance of its founding president. Many left the seemingly hopeless labor to pursue other occupations, but César remained. He persevered with the same principles and dedication that he had brought to farm-labor organizing in the early 1960s.

THE TEAMSTER CHALLENGE

The first major struggle of the 1970s was with the Teamsters, a union dominated by ruthless leaders trying to increase their power. The Teamsters had several times before threatened to expand their operations to organize field workers. In 1970, the Teamsters and the UFW were both members of the AFL-CIO, so the move the Teamsters made in the Salinas area amounted to a raid on the UFW's jurisdiction. The Teamsters had signed sweetheart contracts giving the vegetable growers almost all that they wanted, sacrificing workers' benefits. There was plenty of evidence of collusion. The Teamsters had signed the contracts without even negotiating wage rates for the workers.

Quickly Chávez organized to counter. The UFW staff temporarily moved the headquarters of the union to Salinas and began to organize a strike. Chávez traveled to the AFL-CIO convention in Chicago and attempted, without success, to get the national organization publicly to condemn the Teamsters. Instead the AFL-CIO leadership, led by Bill Kircher, decided informally to pressure the Teamster leadership into withdrawing from the fields. The Teamsters were given to understand that expulsion from the federation was possible for their raid on another union's jurisdiction.

Back in California, César had to improvise to meet challenges as they arose. When a Salinas judge issued a restraining order prohibiting picketing, César protested by going on a fast. His health rapidly deteriorated and he was forced to end the fast after six days.

Some time later, in early August 1970, following mediation by a bishop's committee led by Monsignor Roger Mahony and George Higgins, the Teamsters agreed to withdraw from the fields but not the food-processing sheds where they traditionally had represented workers. This agreement was signed. The Teamsters also secretly agreed to rescind their contracts with the growers and to persuade the employers to renegotiate with the UFW. By August 11, however, the agreement broke down, largely through the hostile actions of the local Teamster boss, Bill Grami, who refused to rescind the Teamster contracts and charged that Chávez had broken the agreement by continuing the UFW's strikes. The growers also dragged their feet, wanting to keep the favorable terms they had gotten from the Teamsters. They were unwilling to accept the UFW terms.

Throughout August, César had selectively picketed the largest corporations, to keep the pressure on the growers with Teamster contracts. Some growers—Inter Harvest, Fresh Pict, Pic 'N' Pac—eventually signed with the UFW. There remained, however, about 170 firms who refused to switch from the Teamsters and Chávez called for a general strike.

THE CHICANO MORATORIUM

The start of the strike coincided with another Chicano event of major proportions. On August 29, five days after Chávez's strike call and the start of all-out organizational war against the Teamsters, Chicano activists organized a massive rally to protest the war in Vietnam. It was billed as a National Chicano Moratorium rally to be held at Laguna Park after a demonstration parade in East Los Angeles.

Other demonstrations against the war by Mexican Americans had preceded this moratorium. Among the many issues of concern was the fact that a disproportionate number of Chicanos were being drafted and killed. Between 1967 and 1969, almost 20 percent of those killed in Vietnam had Spanish surnames—although Mexican Americans made up only about 12 percent of the population of the Southwest and less than 5 percent of the population nationally. César had strong feelings about the war, and organizers of the moratorium approached him. Chávez then wrote to Rosalio Muñoz, one of the organizers of the moratorium march:

> It is now clear to me that the war in Vietnam is gutting the soul of our nation. Of course we know the war to be wrong and unjustifiable, but today we see that it has destroyed the moral fiber of the people.
>
> Our resistance to this, and all war, stems from a deep faith in non-violence. We have to acknowledge that violent warfare between opposing groups—be it over issues of labor or race—is not justifiable. Violence is like acid—it corrodes the movements dedicated to justice.

On 29 August 1970, more than 20,000 people from across the United States met in Los Angeles, paraded down Whittier

Boulevard, and filed into Laguna Park. There were music, food, dances, speeches; cries of *Viva!* and *Raza si, guerra no!* (People yes, war no). In the early afternoon a disturbance nearby at a liquor store provoked a police response that soon led to a riot situation. After ordering the crowd to disburse, more than five hundred helmeted officers charged into the park, chasing some of the protestors who had thrown objects at the police. Tear-gas cannisters were thrown and thousands of people stampeded. Sheriff's deputies rounded up people who had fought back or who had been slow to evacuate the park—hundreds of them—chained them together and maced them repeatedly. Three people were killed: a fifteen-year-old boy, when a tear-gas projectile exploded in his face; a young Chicano, electrocuted after being shot at a police blockade; and a reporter for the *Los Angeles Times*, Ruben Salazar.

Salazar, a long-time critic of the police because of a lack of effective community relations, had taken refuge inside the Silver Dollar Bar on Whittier Boulevard. A sheriff's deputy fired an armor-piercing projectile into the bar, striking Salazar in the head, killing him instantly. Scores of Mexican-American leaders, including César, called for an investigation into the killings and into the police tactics used during the moratorium. A federal grand jury brought an indictment against three officers for violation of Salazar's civil rights, but later they were acquitted of any wrongdoing. A coroner's inquest resulted in a mixed finding of unintended death, and a general feeling by many Chicanos that there was a cover-up.

POLITICAL STRUGGLES

César knew only too well how the police could abuse their power: he had seen it during his years in leading strikes and protests for the farm workers. In Salinas, during the lettuce strike, he saw police beat and harass peaceful picketers and he sympathized with those who considered the moratorium episode as an example of police oppression.

César himself spent most of that December (1970) in a Salinas jail for defying a court injunction against boycotting. A corporation, Bud Antle, Inc., one of the largest growers that opposed a switch from the Teamsters to the UFW, asked a judge in Monterey to order that all boycott activities be stopped. In a dramatic show of nonviolent political resolve, three thousand union supporters silently surrounded the Monterey courthouse when hearings began on 4 December. When Judge Campbell ordered Chávez to jail for contempt, the UFW set up a silent vigil, said daily masses, and sponsored rallies. Ethel Kennedy, Robert Kennedy's widow, and Coretta King, the wife of Dr. Martin Luther King, visited César in his cell. Editorials in the national press called the jailing of Chávez an injustice—and the boycott gained momentum with every article that appeared. On Christmas eve, the state supreme court ordered César released, pending appeal; and in April 1971 the high court ruled in Chávez's favor, finding that the Teamsters had worked in collusion with the growers to oppose the UFW and that the boycott and strike were legal.

In 1971, César moved the union's permanent headquarters from near Delano to an abandoned 300-acre tuberculosis sanitorium in the Tehachapi Mountains near Bakersfield. The former county facility, purchased with the help of a wealthy movie producer, had plenty of room to house the union's many activities as well as provide lodging for the executive board and volunteer workers. Headquarters was now more centrally located, between the two key agricultural regions, the San Joaquin and Imperial Valleys. This cut down on travel time. César also wanted to get away from the interruptions that constantly arose from having the union headquarters located near an urban center and a major highway (the new center was named La Paz—peace). Chávez also felt that the organizers had become too dependent on him for decisions and that the move would promote more local decisionmaking.

In October 1971, César led the union's fight against a farm-labor law that had been passed by the Arizona legislature. Conservative Republicans, aiming to stave off unionization in the fields, supported the law, which outlawed the boycott and limited strikes. To rally opposition to the law and to mobilize farm workers, Chávez began a recall campaign to remove Arizona Governor Jack Williams. In April 1972 he began a fast to raise people's awareness. César fasted for twenty-four days, directing the recall campaign from a small room in Saint Rita's Center in a Mexican barrio in Phoenix. George McGovern, who was running for president, stopped by to visit and lend his encouragement. César explained his fast to Jacques Levy: "The fast is a very personal spiritual thing, and it's not done out of recklessness. It's not done out of a desire to destroy yourself, but it's done out of a deep conviction that we can communicate with people, either those who are for us or against us, faster and more effectively spiritually than we can in any other way."

In the fourth week of the fast, César's heart began to act erratically and he had to be hospitalized. When he ended the fast on 4 June 1972, Joseph Kennedy (Robert Kennedy's son), Joan Baez, and thousands of farm workers attended the mass. The recall campaign fell short by some 108,000 signatures, but in other respects it was successful. At the same time that UFW workers were gathering recall signatures, they were also registering people to vote. These new voters were responsible for electing four Mexican Americans and a Navajo Indian to the state legislature and in helping to elect the first Mexican-American governor in the state's history, Raul Castro. The UFW campaign helped to forge a Chicano-Democrat alliance in Arizona.

That fall, the California growers tried to pass legislation similar to the Arizona measure to hamstring the farm-labor movement. They sponsored Proposition 22, an initiative to outlaw boycotting and limit secret-ballot elections to full-time, nonseasonal employees. Chávez put LeRoy Chatfield in charge of the opposition campaign. César again followed the Arizona strategy of getting citizens registered to vote as well as informing them about the proposition's threat to workers.

He later unearthed fraud in the growers' signature collection for the initiative. The "No on 22" campaign gathered momentum, using human billboards along highways. On 7 November 1972, voters soundly defeated Proposition 22 (58 percent to 42 percent). The UFW had used the boycott organization to mobilize political support and proved they were a serious political force.

THE TEAMSTERS THREATEN AGAIN

For two years (1971 and 1972) California growers refused to recognize either their rescinded Teamster contracts or the UFW's right to succession. The lettuce boycott continued, but Chávez's attention was focused on the political campaigns in Arizona and against Proposition 22. There were signs that the Teamsters had not entirely abandoned the fields and President Nixon's administration encouraged renewed Teamster attacks on the UFW. It was reported that Charles Colson, Nixon's chief counsel, worked with Teamster President Frank Fitzsimmons to hammer out a deal: the Teamster president would support Nixon's reelection, renew the war with the UFW, and testify against some corrupt Teamster officials; in return, the White House would release Jimmy Hoffa from jail and drop legal charges against Fitzsimmons.

On 15 April 1973, after months of stalemated negotiations over new contracts, most of the Coachela and Delano grape growers announced that they had signed contracts with the Teamsters. César immediately called for a strike, pulling out most of the UFW workers from the fields. To intimidate the strikers, the Teamsters recruited five hundred goons from Las Vegas and these toughs, armed with chains, tire-irons, and baseball bats, drove along the picket lines threatening violence. At this, the president of the Seafarers Union, Paul Hall, and fifty muscular seamen joined the UFW ranks. Said Hall, "You got to break those bastards' legs. That's the only thing they understand." On 27 June, the Modesto-based Gallo Winery

signed a contract with the Teamsters. César announced a boycott of all Gallo wines.

Throughout June and July, violence erupted sporadically in
the strike area: beatings, shootings, stabbings, a bombing,
and arson. On 23 June, 180 Teamsters attacked the UFW picket
lines with machetes, iron pipes, and baseball bats. The melee
lasted an hour and left twenty-five persons injured. Eleven
people were arrested—five UFW members and six Teamsters.
Grami announced that the Teamsters would withdraw all their
"guards" from the picket lines, beginning 5 July, but the violence continued. Late that summer, two union members were
killed: an immigrant from Yemen, Nergi Daifulla, on 14 August, and sixty-year-old Juan de la Cruz on 16 August. César,
deeply upset by the deaths of two loyal unionists, called on all
union members to fast for three days. He told Levy that "It
must be a time to think again about violence and nonviolence."

On 1 September, César called off the strike and resumed the
boycott. The decision was motivated in part by his desire to
avoid future violence, but also because he deeply felt that a
boycott would be more effective than a strike. The seasonal
pattern of migrant farm labor meant that in the fall there
would be fewer workers for the picket lines: it was time to
switch to the tried-and-true tactic of the boycott. But the
situation was not good. The union had lost 90 percent of its
contracts to the Teamsters and membership had shrunk from
40,000 to 6,500. More than 3,500 union members and supporters had been arrested; and the union's $1.6 million strike
loan from the AFL-CIO was exhausted.

At the union's constitutional convention in late September,
414 delegates drafted a formal constitution for the United
Farm Workers of America, AFL-CIO. In part, this was to
improve the union's bureaucratic machinery, but César also
wanted to enable the farm workers to reaffirm their support
for the union. He thought the convention would strengthen
the members' flagging strength. There were marathon meet-

Chávez at rostrum during the UFW's 1973 Constitutional Convention. Leonard Woodcock of the AFL–CIO is at far right.

ings—the convention took place in Fresno's new convention center—and hundreds of spectators filled the galleries. Speeches by VIP supporters (among them Senator Edward Kennedy and Leonard Woodcock, the UAW president) punctuated the debates.

The III-page constitution adopted did not distinguish between citizen and noncitizen members. The purpose of the union was defined as "to unite under its banner all individuals employed as agricultural laborers, regardless of race, creed, sex or nationality." The constitution provided for a Bill of

Dolores Huerta and César Chávez at the UFW's 1973 Constitutional
Convention.

Rights for all members, regardless of citizenship or legal status in the United States. All members had the right to participate equally in union affairs and to benefit from union services (the UFW had more than thirty service centers in California: members received help with problems ranging from rent disputes to immigration advice). In the matter of helping members, there was a significant difference in approach between the UFW and the Teamsters. In the UFW, a union center was a place where farm workers could go to learn how and when to claim state and federal benefits. In addition, union members had a pension plan (to which the employers contributed), a credit union offering low-interest loans, a number of UFW clinics with low-cost medical treatment, including dentistry, a low-cost retirement home, and prepaid legal services. All this was an outgrowth of the *mutualista* concept of service and self help that Chávez had fostered from the beginning of the union in 1962. Teamster members, on the other hand, had none of these benefits. The difference underscored the fact that the Teamsters was a company union.

Twice in 1974 the Teamsters indicated willingness to sign a peace pact, largely at the insistence of the AFL-CIO leadership. The AFL-CIO wanted an end to the boycott: it was hurting their relations with non-farm-worker unionists. Both times, however, the Teamsters broke the jurisdictional agreements almost as soon as they were negotiated.

The end of the Teamster threat to the UFW came largely because of Teamster internal disputes and the mysterious disappearance of Jimmy Hoffa (his body was never found). The Nixon White House, its energies focused on the Watergate crisis, no longer could be depended upon for support. But this did not signal plain sailing for the UFW. Even though in late 1974 the Teamsters finally gave up their campaign to organize field workers and take over UFW contracts, many grape and vegetable growers had contracts in place that did not expire for several years. Meantime, César had to decide on a strategy to keep his union together.

THE CALIFORNIA FARM LABOR ACT

In 1975 Chávez intensified the boycott of Gallo wines (the AFL-CIO had agreed to support the UFW lettuce and grape boycotts if the UFW would drop its secondary boycott of Safeway and A&P markets). Gallo had signed a Teamsters contract after a contract it had had with the UFW expired. The winery was highly vulnerable.

On 22 February, César and supporters of the UFW started a 110-mile march from San Francisco to Gallo's home winery in Modesto. More than 15,000 were in the march when it ended, a week later. The tremendous turn-out again proved that the UFW had great popular support and the boycott reinvigorated a sense that the union had political strength beyond the issue of contracts. The message was not lost on California's new governor, Jerry Brown. Son of the former governor, Pat Brown, and educated at a Roman Catholic seminary, Jerry was an ascetic figure. Some considered him to be almost an antipolitician, a perfect type to succeed in the post-Watergate era. Jerry Brown had supported the farm workers' cause and marched with them in the Coachella Valley. As California's secretary of state in 1972, he had helped the UFW challenge Proposition 22. His election to the governorship in November 1974 had signaled a new opportunity for Chávez.

In 1974 César began to think that a state agricultural law might help reverse the decline of the union's strength, but only if the law had certain provisions. First, it had to allow for boycotts. The background to this aspect went back many years: the growers had periodically proposed versions of a law to regulate labor strife in the fields, since farm workers were exempt from the National Labor Relations Act. For the UFW, this exemption had both positive and negative results. On the negative side, the government did not have to take responsibility for enforcing fair elections and representation (and a result of this was the years of fighting with the Teamsters). On the positive side, exclusion from the NLRA meant that the

UFW was also exempt from the anti–secondary boycott provisions of that law and its successors. César had rejected and fought against attempts to include farm workers under the NLRA or previous state-sponsored labor laws, precisely because they outlawed what he considered his most powerful organizing tactic—the boycott.

Second, Chávez wanted any new state law to allow seasonal workers to vote in labor elections. Under previously proposed legislation—including that in Arizona—only permanent workers would have been allowed to vote. Third, a UFW-supported farm-labor law had to allow for legitimate strikes. Initially the growers opposed all these conditions, but by 1975, after the years of strikes, jurisdictional violence, and boycotts, they were willing to negotiate.

In late 1974, Richard Alatorre, a newly elected Democrat from Los Angeles who was also a UFW supporter, introduced a farm-labor bill with the backing of Chávez and the union. It had been drafted with input from Chávez and Jack Henning, head of the California AFL-CIO. Now the endorsement of the new governor was needed. Brown's top aide working on the bill was LeRoy Chatfield, a former UFW staff member, and although Alatorre's bill did not pass the legislature, a modified version of it passed the next year. Governor Brown supported it and mediated between the factions.

The California Agricultural Labor Relations Act (May 1975) was the first law governing farm-labor organizing in the continental United States (Hawaii had a similar law). The California law—an outgrowth of the events set in motion by the lettuce strike and boycott of August 1970—was a compromise. But it gave César what he wanted: secret ballot elections, the right to boycott, voting rights for migrant seasonal workers, and control over the timing of elections. The growers, for their part, were convinced that the law would end the boycotts and labor disruptions that had cost them millions of dollars.

A month after the passage of the law, César intensified both the boycott and the union's organizing efforts. He wanted to expedite the coming union-recognition elections. Starting out from Calexico, on the Mexican border, he led what was to be a thousand-mile march through the Imperial and San Joaquin Valleys. Each night—for fifty-nine days—Chávez spoke at rallies along the way, advertising the upcoming elections. Meanwhile, the Teamsters continued to organize farm workers in opposition to the UFW.

The first elections took place on 28 August 1975, amidst charges of voter fraud and intimidation by the growers. After a month of elections, the Teamsters and UFW had an even split, 74 victories for the UFW and 73 for the Teamsters. But by the end of 1975, the UFW took the lead with 198 contracts (representing 27,000 workers) to the Teamsters' 115 contracts (12,000 workers). The continued strength of the Teamsters largely resulted from the growers' tactics. The Teamsters were allowed special access, workers were threatened, and UFW members fired. The Immigration Service was called to get rid of UFW votes among illegal workers. The UFW filed more than one thousand complaints alleging violation of the new law's election provisions. More than 80 percent of the elections were challenged.

Governor Brown continued to support Chávez and the UFW, appointing a pro-UFW majority to the Agricultural Labor Relations Board (ALRB), the body that supervised the elections. On the five-member board were former organizer LeRoy Chatfield, Roger Mahony, the auxiliary bishop of Fresno who had worked with the UFW, and two liberal Democrats. These appointments infuriated the growers, who initiated lawsuits and legislative maneuvering to weaken the board.

One controversy was over access to the workplace. The UFW wanted unlimited right to enter ranches and farms to talk to workers about the union; the growers wanted control over access, which would give preference to the Teamsters. Growers posted armed guards at entrances to their farms to prevent UFW organizers from entering. Another problem was

ALRB funding. At the beginning of 1976, the board ran out of money for its daily operation. Operations were suspended for five months until the legislature could vote for a regular appropriation. Since in the legislature there was not the necessary majority to pass an emergency appropriation, the ALRB stopped reviewing and certifying elections.

Fighting back on both issues, César decided to appeal to California's voters. In a massive initiative campaign, UFW workers gathered more than 700,000 signatures in only twenty-nine days. The initiative, known as Proposition 14, was to be voted on in November 1976. It would guarantee adequate funding for the ALRB and free access for union organizers. The ease with which the union got the signatures for the initiative scared the growers into deciding to defuse the issue by supporting funding for the ALRB. They wanted to focus on the access issue.

César personally directed the UFW campaign. He put all available volunteers on the campaign to promote Proposition 14—but the opposition rallied massive support. A huge media campaign, funded by oil companies and land corporations, spent $1.8 million to tell the voters, deceptively, that the initiative was a threat to everyone's property rights. Despite endorsements by Jerry Brown and presidential candidate Jimmy Carter, Proposition 14 lost by a two to one margin.

WIN SOME, LOSE SOME

Jimmy Carter won the 1976 presidential election, but the next decade or so—with Reagan as the next resident in the White House—was to see a change in public mood. And the defeat of Proposition 14 in California may have been the turning point for Chávez's ability to mobilize public support for the farm workers. The UFW, deprived of adequate access to the workers, could no longer rely on the Farm Labor Board for help in organizing farm workers. The conservative mood in the state resulted in the appointment of pro-grower representatives on the Farm Labor Board. They consistently ruled against the union in the many grievances that were brought before it. Moreover, the labor law did not require that the growers sign contracts: only that they bargain with the election winners. The UFW might win an election and then be tied up in interminable negotiations over the contract—their only weapon, the strike.

The nation would soon take on a conservative mood under the Republican administrations of Ronald Reagan, which meant a decline in public support for labor unions in general as well as a lessening of concern for the plight of the farm workers. There had been victories, however. One had come in 1975, the result of years of lobbying and complex legal manueuvers: the abolition of *el cortito,* the short-handled hoe. For decades the growers had required field workers to use this tool that demanded its user bend over while working. Thousands of farm workers damaged their backs and spent the rest of their lives in disabling pain. Chávez and the UFW opposed the use of this hoe and with attorneys for California Rural Legal Aid (CRLA), campaigned to outlaw it. After lengthy government hearings, a Supreme Court ruling (*Sebastian Carmona et al. vs. Division of Industrial Safety* 1975), and a 1975 California administrative ruling, the short-handled hoe was outlawed.

For all the disappointment at the defeat of Prop. 14, the period following the passage of the California Farm Labor Act was one of growth in membership and number of contracts. The UFW had won almost two-thirds of the elections after 1975, and the Teamsters admitted in March 1977 that they were beaten. They would not contest future elections. The dues-paying membership of the UFW soared to more than 100,000 by 1978, and effective strikes resulted in contracts in the Santa Maria Valley and in the Imperial Valley. Chávez also continued the union's policy of forging alliances with other unions; for instance, the UFW joined with a Puerto Rican farm-workers' union and with the Farm Labor Organizing Committee in the Midwest.

Dolores Huerta and César continued to have a great deal of

influence within the California legislature. Some of their proposals became laws: in addition to the measure banning el
cortito, another new law improved worker-compensation for
field workers. By 1978, Chávez announced that the grape and
lettuce boycotts were over and that henceforth the union
would boycott only selective labels.

The union had reached a degree of organizational success,
but there were troubling signs of division. A number of long-
time staff members quit the union, some expressing unhappi-
ness with César's leadership. Others admitted to being burned
out by the long hours at almost no pay. In March 1981, Jerry
Cohen, the UFW's chief attorney, left for personal reasons, to
spend more time with his family. Tensions within the union
had made it impossible for him to continue. A few months later
Marshall Ganz, who had helped to organize the lettuce strike,
and Jim Drake, along with a number of other union leaders
from the Salinas area, left the union over a dispute having to
do with the selection of union representatives. Chávez contended that the dissidents were attempting to undermine his
leadership by opposing his choices to the union board. The
Salinas dissidents went on a hunger strike to protest their re-
moval by Chávez, and the union filed a $25 million libel suit
against them. The print media reaction was to magnify these
resignations into a signal that this spelled the end for the
Chávez-led union. The *Village Voice* ran a two-part series entitled "César Chávez's Fall from Grace," supposedly exposing
internal dissention in the union.

After the defeat of Proposition 14, César decided to reorga-
nize the union. In his words: "The world was really changing.
Now we had to start planning. We had to talk about restruc-
turing the union. We had to look at what we were doing."
Even before the defeat of Proposition 14, in late 1975, he had
called for a conference to discuss ideas for modernizing the
union. Later he invited Kenneth Blanchard, author of *The One-
Minute Manager,* to visit La Paz to give a management seminar.
Blanchard accepted and did the session free of charge. César

invited other consultants to the union headquarters, and the staff began discussing new ideas. Said César, "I loved it. We talked about planning and doing studies. I mean we were above normal." As part of the modernization drive during the late 1970s, they computerized the union records and purchased a microwave communications system that made them no longer dependent on public telephones. César also experimented with techniques of interpersonal communication borrowed from Synanon, the drug dependency/recovery program whose controversial director, Charles Diedrick, César had known since the 1950s.

César wanted to decentralize the union. The plan was to create five groups within the UFW, each group to be responsible for its own budgeting and programs. Privately he hoped that he could develop leadership that would not be so dependent on his decisionmaking. Marshall Ganz and the elected UFW representatives in Salinas, however, felt that César was not willing enough to delegate power. Some departing UFW staff claimed that the Synanon communication "game" pitted them against each other and caused bad feelings among people. Newspaper editorials leveled charges that Chávez had given up traditional organizing activities in favor of electronic mass-mailings. Others criticized the move from Forty Acres to La Paz, saying it isolated the union. César was said to have centralized the leadership of the union too much; he was acting like a dictator. Chávez and the UFW leadership denied all these charges and the UFW successfully sued some critics for libel, but dissident accounts in the press continued and César was accused of not being a good administrator. This became a vicious circle: published attacks on the effectiveness of his leadership were followed by a wane in union membership.

Internal division and criticism were not all. In 1979, César got involved on the losing end of a political battle over the selection of a speaker for the California Assembly. A long-time UFW supporter from Los Angeles, Democrat Howard Berman, was running for the position against Willie Brown, another Democrat, from San Francisco. At stake was the UFW's political influence in the Assembly: as speaker, Berman would be able to influence key appointments to the Farm Labor Board. César had promises from two Chicano Assemblymen, Art Torres and Richard Alatorre, initially to support Berman during the voting; but both Torres and Alatorre switched when, in a final vote, Brown appeared to be going to win. César, taking this to be betrayal, was enraged. Eventually, Alatorre appeared before a UFW convention to apologize for his vote, but Torres was unrepentant, and when he ran for reelection César supported his opponent, Alex Garcia. Garcia nevertheless lost. Torres in turn retaliated, rejecting UFW-supported candidates for the Farm Labor Board, and as a result Republican Governor George Deukmejian was able to appoint to the board people hostile to the UFW. The struggle seemed further to diminish the political capital of the UFW.

By the 1980s, the UFW had lost its earlier momentum. In 1984, only fifteen of the seventy grape growers in the Delano area were under a UFW contract. The union was winning fewer and fewer elections: in 1976 it had won 276, but in the years since it had won a total of only 56. Union membership dropped from a high of more than 30,000 to less than 12,000 active members. Fewer and fewer strikes occurred, and the UFW reduced the number of organizers in the fields, hoping to encourage local leadership and initiative. This brought renewed criticism from former allies and friends. Chávez was accused of abandoning organizing in the fields. César countered that in those cases where the union did organize workers and hold elections, final recognition and contracts were not forthcoming. The growers, he said, manipulated the Farm Labor Board and used the tactic of shifting the ownership of ranches once a contract had been negotiated. With the state government machinery turned against the union, strikes and on-site organizing were wasted effort. The real answer to the decline in union membership and contracts, César thought,

was the Farm Labor Board's prejudice toward grower interests. The board was being used to stifle unionization.

On the average, the ALRB took 348 days to settle disputes
over contested elections and about half as long to render a
decision whether to litigate an unfair labor practice. By 1984,
after almost ten years of existence, the ALRB had not made
a single award for violation of the labor law. The decline in
organizing power in the fields was due to the tremendous
economic and political power of the giant multinationals in
California, compounded by internal divisions within the UFW.

The stalemate promoted by the ALRB and dwindling union
strength forced César to conclude that the only tactic left was
to renew the boycott to pressure the growers to sign contracts. On 12 June 1984 he announced that the union would
embark on a new grape boycott. However, over the years the
UFW had sponsored more than fifty boycotts and the public
was confused as to what was and what was not boycotted. A
tremendous educational campaign was needed. Chávez called
for a modern strategy: "We will use modern techniques of direct mailings, media advertising and other means of once
again bringing together liberals, church groups, workers and
others to support us until the full meaning of the California
labor law is restored and provides protections workers must
have." It was to be a high-tech boycott, relying on computer-
generated mailings, slick advertising, and media packets. César
believed the most sensitive issue of appeal to consumers was
that of pesticide-residues on fruit.

The union first became aware of the dangers of pesticides in
the summer of 1968 when farm workers had gone to the UFW's
clinics with symptoms of pesticide poisoning. The union researched the dangers of pesticides to the workers and consumers. In 1969, when the union renegotiated its first grape
contracts with Perelli-Minetti, they contained very strong pesticide clauses, regulating pesticide use and the amount of ex-
posure permitted for workers. Thereafter, from the time of the

first grape boycott, union flyers and advertisements warned consumers that only union-label grapes could be guaranteed as being safe from pesticide residues. In the 1970s, the strong pesticide clauses demanded by the UFW were one of the main stumbling blocks preventing the growers from negotiating with the UFW.

During the 1980s, Chávez targeted the environmental concerns of the nation's middle class. The UFW produced a movie, *The Wrath of Grapes,* in which graphic footage showed birth defects and high rates of cancer produced by pesticide poisoning among farm workers and consumers. In 1987 and 1988, César traveled to cities in the Midwest and the East where grape consumption was viewed as a luxury item and where union support had always been the strongest. His speeches were recorded in the local papers. In Lansing, Michigan, referring to his environmental emphasis, César told his audience: "Ten to fifteen years ago we were aiming at the whole population. Now we've done our homework and we know who we're talking to." In Champaign, Illinois, Chávez explained that the boycott was the most effective way to get growers to change their use of pesticides in general: "There are more reported pesticide poisonings with grapes than with any other type of produce," he told them. "We don't have the resources to try and boycott other types of produce." In Austin, Texas, where Chávez visited a group of elementary school children and showed the film, the children marched around the school carrying the UFW banner and posters saying, "Keep our food clean."

On 16 July 1988, at La Paz, César started a fast to protest pesticide usage. The fast—in which he consumed only water—went largely unnoticed by the public until the children of Robert Kennedy visited La Paz to lend their support. As in the past, the fast became a rallying point for union supporters. Daily bulletins on César's health were issued on the union's radio station, KUFW, and nightly mass was held, with thousands in attendance. Dolores Huerta noted: "This is a spiritual thing with him. This is not a publicity stunt." The fast, more than any other action by César, nevertheless drew attention to the boycott and the pesticide issue. On Sunday 22 August—after thirty-six days—César ended the fast. As an expression of support, Jesse Jackson, a presidential candidate, and actors Martin Sheen and Robert Blake later fasted for three days to keep alive the "chain of suffering"; and for several months, individuals undertook three-day minifasts to demonstrate their support for the union.

During his fast, César issued a statement that summarized his commitment to the union and the boycott:

> As I look back at this past year, I can see many events that precipitated the fast, including the terrible suffering of farm workers and their children, the crushing of farm worker rights, the denial of fair and free elections and the death of good-faith bargaining in California agriculture. All of these events are connected with the great cause of justice for farm worker families.

Into the 1990s, Chávez exhibited the same qualities of character that had brought him success in the earlier struggles. He was tenacious in his leadership, despite a change in the activist mood of the country. Chávez believed that a modern boycott could be won with an alliance among "Latinos, blacks, and other minorities, plus allies in labor and the Church." He also believed that for the generation of activists from the 1960s and 1970s, the boycott would become "a social habit." Statistics for the crucial period from May to August 1990, when the grape harvest was at its height, seemed to bear out his optimism. Grapes delivered for sale declined in twelve major cities. In New York City, grape consumption was down 74 percent; in Los Angeles it declined by 37 percent; in San Francisco, 36 percent. In 1991 the UFW cited official statistics showing that the growers were selling grapes at a loss and Chávez was confident about the ultimate success of the boycott: "In political campaigns you race against time to get your message out— and you are always dramatically outspent. With boycotts, time becomes your ally. In the end, it can be a more powerful force than all the money that special interests can muster." If history was to be a guide, the success of the boycott would be assured mainly through the hard work of hundreds of dedicated volunteers inspired by the vision put forth by the UFW's leader. César Chávez never gave up on the farm workers.

CHAPTER 8

The Presence, the Spirit, the Fire

The living spirit grows and even outgrows its earlier forms of expression; it freely chooses the men in whom it lives and who proclaim it. This living spirit is eternally renewed and pursues its goal in manifold and inconceivable ways throughout the history of mankind.

C. G. JUNG

IN May 1969, César Chávez attended a breakfast at a downtown hotel in El Paso, Texas, to which a cross section of the Mexicanos in that city was invited. Represented were numerous Mexican-American organizations: the League of United Latin American Citizens (LULAC), the Mexican-American Youth Organization (MAYO), the Movimiento Estudiantil Chicano de Aztlan (MECHA), and the Alianza (a South El Paso Barrio youth group with ties to Reies López Tijerina of New Mexico). Others present included local Mexican-American politicians, university professors, teachers, community leaders, students, and farm workers, as well as Anglo-American friends of the farm workers. Chávez, seeking support for the United Farm Workers Organizing Committee, was in the middle of a struggle against multinational agribusinesses. The current issues were the grape strike and the promotion of Chávez's innovative secondary boycotts.

A wave of meetings had set up committees of "Friends" throughout the country—basically, Anglo-American groups of religious, union, academic, and student supporters. These support groups were ideologically shaped by a liberal consciousness: support for workers' rights, civil rights, and social justice. The overall feeling was one of goodwill for the downtrodden. In the late 1960s, these liberals were not only outraged that the United States government subsidized agribusiness, they were protesting the Defense Department's increased purchases of grapes—a government effort to offset the consumer boycotts. They saw these moves as similar to the government's role in Vietnam: oppressive.

The Mexican Americans at the breakfast meeting in El Paso had, in addition, another reason for attending; they wanted to feel the presence of their lost "soul." Chávez gave them solace in a world where they often felt alienated and powerless. For many he represented their lost sensitivity to the land, their past, their traditions. Regardless of ideological orientation, the Mexicanos at the meeting felt the presence of a lost *Mexicanidad*. They were constructing a new spiritual reality around a man who, for the most part, just listened. Nobody said so, but many perceived Chávez as a spiritual rather than a political leader—a savior in their midst.

For the Chicanos at the breakfast, Chávez's spirituality was the central theme, intertwined as the meeting was with the symbols of religion and motherhood: Our Lady of Guadalupe and the farm workers' flag. Many of them felt this central core of a shared Mexicanidad: Indianism, immigration, spirituality, historical struggle, the quest for freedom from oppression. In the words of essayist Richard Rodriguez (writing in 1991): "Chávez wielded a spiritual authority that, if it was political at all, it was not mundane and had to be exerted in large, priestly ways or it was squandered. César Chávez was a folk hero."

Throughout the Southwest, Chávez had become synonymous with La Causa; and La Causa was each Mexicano's need for redemption from modernity. When the question was asked, "César, when will you become the leader of the Chicano movement?" the mood of the meeting changed: it was now political, ideological, temporal. The meeting returned to concrete realities and problems. Nevertheless, Chávez had touched everyone at the meeting in a deeply spiritual way. He had, for a moment, inspired a new hope; an innocent faith in possibility. Chávez's touch was not Corky Gonzales's political-historicalism (see his poem, "I am Joaquin"); nor was it the revolutionary vision of Reies López Tijerina, struggling for land in Tierra Amarilla; certainly not the pragmatic, third-party strategy of José Angel Gutiérrez's Raza Unida Party. It was more a vision of a pastoral past blessed by the Virgin of Guadalupe. If Chávez's presence was meaningful as a new symbolic representation of the Mexican-American/Chicano soul, it was as interpreted through his organizational message.

The ideological view of the farm workers was framed in the text of the "Proclamation of the Delano Grape Workers for International Boycott," published in *El Malcriado* on 15–30 April 1969. This read:

> We have been farm workers for hundreds of years and pioneers for seven. Mexicans, Filipinos, Africans and others, our ancestors were among those who founded this land and tamed its natural wilderness. But we are still pilgrims on this land and, and we are pioneers who blaze a trail out of the wilderness of hunger and deprivation that we have suffered even as our ancestors did. We are conscious today of the significance of our present quest. If this road we chart leads to the rights and reforms we demand, if it leads to just wages, humane working conditions, protection from the misuse of pesticides, and to the fundamental right of collective bargaining, if it changes the social order that relegates us to the bottom reaches of society, then in our wake will follow thousands of American farm workers. Our example will make them free.

Unfortunately, as Richard Rodriguez accurately pointed out, "by the late 1970s, Chávez had spent his energies in legislative maneuvers. His union got mixed up in a power struggle with the Teamsters. Criticized in the liberal press for allowing his union to unravel, Chávez became a quixotic figure, Gandhi without an India." Chávez did not accept the Chicano poet Alurista's mythical Aztlan, nor the militant new Chicano multiculturalism without Americanism.

MEXICAN AMERICANS TO CHICANOS

In the early 1960s, Mexican-American intellectuals had established a new, ethnic, social context for Mexican Americans that set the stage for the emergence of César Chávez. At a 1965 conference headed by Julián Samora, a leading Mexican-American intellectual, the socioeconomic and intellectual conditions of the Mexican-American community were analyzed. Out of this conference came *La Raza: Forgotten Americans* (1966). It dealt with the problems of *la raza:* the inferior conditions endured by Mexican Americans, limiting their possibilities for freedom and equality. In many ways the ideas that Chávez and young Chicanos used in the years following were those that had been set out in the early 1960s.

Scholars and political leaders such as George Sánchez, Ernesto Galarza, Eduardo Quevedo, Eugene Gonzalez, Bernardo Valdez, Julián Samora, and others met at Notre Dame University and later in San Francisco to discuss the themes that would shape the Spanish-speaking communities. During the conference, educator George Sánchez emphasized the persistence of the Spanish language. That, he said, was the key to a continuing consciousness of *Lo Mexicano.* John A. Wagner, a clergyman, emphasized the theme of spirituality. He specifically underscored three basic connections within the Spanish-speaking mind: poverty, spirituality, and religious diversity. Catholicism, he said, was predominant, but Protestantism (in its various forms) was also central, because it linked a ministry of spirituality with one of economic help. Wagner emphasized that Mexicanos (the most favored term in the early 1960s) in the United States found something lacking in the U.S. Catholic Church. It did not meet the needs of their spirituality—a soul that thrived on an interrelationship of leadership, hope, and trust. Chávez later met this need.

In the early 1960s, political scientist John Martínez had noted that, with the exception of the union leadership, most Mexican-American leaders were middle-class. Neither the unions nor organizations such as the Mexican-American Political Association (MAPA), the Political Association of Spanish Speaking Organizations (PASSO), the Community Service Organization (CSO), American G.I. Forum, and (the oldest and strongest) the League of United Latin American Citizens (LULAC) had a spiritual core or philosophy that reached every Mexican American. Earlier (in the 1930s and into the 1950s) LULAC had had aspects of this, but by the late 1950s and early 1960s it had lost much of its "spiritual" and political potential. Young Chicano professionals in the late 1970s reenergized it.

Many Mexican Americans perceived the organizations listed above as competing regional bodies without the potential to be national in scope. These organizations, along with most of the prominent politicos of the early 1960s (e.g., Henry B. Gonzalez of Texas, Edward Roybal of California, Kiki de la Garza of Texas, Henry Montoya of New Mexico) did not have a national presence. Until César Chávez emerged in the mid-1960s, there was no Martin Luther King Jr. in Mexican-American politics. In 1966, Spanish-speakers had not given up their distrust of politicians, their faith in the importance of soul, their sense of community over individualism, their historical ethnic memory, kept alive by new waves of Mexican immigrants. And they had not lost their idealization of leadership. The subprocesses of assimilation were undoubtedly occurring in Mexican-American communities, but ethnicity persisted because of a number of factors: immigration, prejudice, poverty, and the nominal biculturalism of the Southwest.

By 1966, with the rise of César Chávez and the farm workers' struggle, the stage was set for the emergence of new leaders, what historians Matt Meier and Feliciano Rivera termed *the four horsemen:* César Chávez, Reies López Tijerina, Corky Gonzales, and José Angel Gutiérrez. All four of these leaders acquired national reputations among Chicano youth by the late 1960s, but only Chávez had the reputation and support that crossed class and generational as well as regional lines. Chávez and his farm workers' struggle appealed to all Mexicanos, regardless of class, region, or ideology. This new leadership saw itself as being completely responsible to the Spanish-speaking communities and their issues. These new leaders, therefore, met the general criteria of the Mexicano communities—a leadership that conceived of itself as at one with the "folk society," but that was also able to address the issues of modernity, poverty, power, identity, and property (land) within the larger United States society. True, the "four horsemen" concept appealed to young Chicanos, but even without the others Chávez commanded respect, loyalty, and support beyond his immediate region.

This new leadership fit the goals of the 1965 Mexican-American think tank mentioned above. The conference's main organizers, Herman Gallegos, Lyle Saunders, and Julián Samora, had specifically seen the need for a new kind of ethnic leadership. These leaders should be directly responsive to the needs of Mexican-American communities, address common goals, be problem-solving in orientation, and provide a leadership that emanated specifically from Spanish-speaking traditions. Above all, the Samora group thought that "although the Spanish-speaking must continue to provide leadership, this does not mean that others [Anglo-Americans] should not be encouraged to make political, financial, and other contributions, but that this should not preclude the Spanish-speaking from raising funds within their own group before seeking support from others." The Samora group believed that leadership could be financed principally by national foundations. At the same time it emphasized "aggressive programs of community organizations and political action." The group stated in their report: "The foundations must extend their aid to the struggling minorities as they have never done to increase their opportunities for maximum participation in our society. Foundations should also give financial assistance to action programs that cannot be advanced through federal funding."

It turned out that Chávez was the only leader during the 1960s who commanded the status to receive major institutional contributions and donations (the others of the four in any case did not accept corporate donations because of ideological considerations). Chávez was the only one of the four to seek a basic program of economic and structural integration for all Mexicans in the United States, and his acceptance of the mainstream had a tremendous appeal to most Mexican Americans, Anglo-American supporters, and financial backers. Chávez never lashed out at "white capitalist" America.

Interestingly, in view of how things turned out, the Samora group warned against leadership being siphoned off into poverty programs: "[ethnic] leaders at all levels might be converted from social-protest activists to persons providing only social service." Rodolfo Acuña, in his *Occupied America*, later lamented that such a trend actually developed. Effective change for the Samora group meant a transformation implemented by a leadership responsible solely to Spanish-speaking communities, not to agencies or institutions. In addition, the changes must be for the masses, not just for those "groups that are proficient in writing proposals and display sophisticated grantsmanship [and] are the ones that secure funds rather than the more disadvantaged and less sophisticated groups." The major concern of Samora et al. was that training for the resident poor would not be available if community leaders were moved out of the barrios. Samora's group disagreed with the solutions proposed in President Lyndon Johnson's poverty programs. As they wrote in *La Raza: Forgotten Americans:* "One result of the anti-poverty program has been the recruiting of leaders into federal staffs, with loss of time, interest, and energy to the local Spanish-speaking communities." The Samora group believed that Mexican Americans needed self-help through their own leadership, not welfare help through government leadership.

Clearly, the Mexican-American middle class and intellectuals saw the need in the early 1960s for indigenous leadership. But the intellectuals, politicians, and activists in the Samoran group feared not only government-influenced leadership; they also warned against excessively ideological leaders. The philosophy of the leaders, they believed, must be embedded in traditional values. The generation of the immediate postwar period, with its desire for full participation in the American way of life, was pronouncing a new direction: a leadership that needed ethnic "presence." They envisioned a Mexican-American Franklin Roosevelt with the added qualities of Mexican President Lázaro Cárdenas. This cry for a new leader and a new era sought community not individualism, leadership not civil servants, justice not welfare or political revolution, and meaningful integration not prideful separation. The 1960s Mexican-American intellectuals sought to return to an ethnicity based on *Lo Mexicano*, not to incorporate a radical, Third World nationalism. They wrote: "The Spanish-speaking population has reached a stage in its development where its influence is being felt in local, regional, and national matters. Private and public agencies at all levels are ready to listen to the ideas and even demands that [this group] is ready to express." This new intellectual context was receptive to Chávez's leadership. The new *grito* (cry) was for an ethnic "presence."

CHÁVEZ AND PERSONAL MAGNETISM

In the early 1960s, many middle-class Mexican Americans were not acquainted with César Chávez. The first voice they heard interpreting Chávez was that of Eugene Nelson, a close follower and associate of Chávez's and early member of the farm workers' union. In *Huelga: The First Hundred Days of the Great Delano Grape Strike* (1966), Nelson addressed Chávez's anonymity directly. In a section entitled "Who is Chávez?" Nelson portrayed the union leader "as a man scarred by prejudice, highly intelligent, and extremely aware—in almost a poetic sense—of everything in life." Nelson characterized Chávez as "a man with a healthy sense of his own worth and with a corresponding intense drive to see that he and his kind are treated as equals; yet, he has a disarming simplicity, down-to-earthness, and interest in the ordinary things of life." Mexican Americans and academics reading Nelson's text (or excerpts, in Manuel P. Servin's *The Mexican-Americans: An Awakening Minority*, 1970) began to get a feeling for César Chávez. He was, they believed, a man who was honest, who had a strong sense of the work ethic, who was dedicated not only to his family but to the community of farm workers, and who had a strong desire to bring equality, respect, and justice to all Mexicans, especially the poorest of them. Chávez seemed to fit the ticket, not only for the Mexican-American middle class but also for the radical young Chicano activists and the working class.

Nelson astutely stated that Chávez had "a great deal of personal magnetism . . . as well as an undeniably keen intelligence and exceedingly pleasant if not handsome appearance," adding: "He is one of those persons one feels [one] has known all [one's] life." Because of his close and strong alliance to Chávez, Nelson attempted to give voice to the actual sentiments and thoughts of the farm workers. According to Nelson, the farm workers had seen what Samora and his group had wanted in leadership: a man of, for, and by the people. "There is no one else of his stature in sight in the Mexican community," wrote Nelson.

Chávez also seemed to be the answer to the problem of lack of leadership posed by José Antonio Villarreal (author of the first Chicano novel, *Pocho*) when, in 1966, he addressed the issue of "Mexican-Americans and the Leadership Crisis" in the *Los Angeles Times West Magazine*. Villarreal, like other Mexican-American intellectuals of the early sixties, sought viable leadership. Chávez seemed to fill a perceived vacuum.

Historian Rodolfo Acuña later addressed this quest for a leader from the point of view of the labor unions. He chronicled the growing importance of Mexicans and Mexican Americans within the U.S. labor movement. Chávez, as Acuña observed, was rooted in the major sector of the Mexican-American working class and supported by a major "foundation"—the unions.

By the middle to late 1960s, Chávez was perceived as a union man, an activist, a leader in class struggles, a pluralist power broker, a religious teacher, a fighter for social justice, and as "the last of the Jeffersonians." Each person and each movement had found its own Chávez. But all had felt the same power in the spirit of his presence. Middle-class Mexicans especially applauded his insistence on nonviolence, at a time when black and white student militancy was on the rise. They also applauded his humanism.

The theme of social and economic justice appealed not only to the middle class but to religious communities—an aspect of Chávez that came out of the lessons he took from Father McDonnell on the teachings of Pope Leo XIII's papal encyclicals. Teachings about social responsibility and economic justice also flavored the organizing methodology and techniques of Saul Alinsky's Industrial Areas Foundation that Chávez acquired from his mentor Fred Ross. Alinsky's philosophy of nonviolence was issue-oriented, anti-Communist, grassroots-oriented, and nonideological; it was pragmatic and prodemocratic, resting on a philosophical fulcrum of justice, civic virtue, and empowerment of the people. To this, Chávez added a religious base: faith, supported by the rituals, symbols, and authority of the Roman Catholic Church, a religiosity central to the traditions of many Mexicans.

Richard Rodriguez (1991) believed that Chávez had engaged in a Quixotic venture. Acuña, one of the most widely read radical/activist historians of the 1960s and 1970s and champion of Movimiento Estudiantil Chicano de Aztlan (MECHA), a student organization, believed that Chávez was, like himself, a person who did not engage in "Quixotic fights" (Acuña's term), but constantly struggled for the Chicano movement. Rodriguez perceived Chávez as a metaphor for spirit in his book, *Days of Obligation* (1991). Acuña, on the other hand, in

Occupied America (1978), saw him as a revolutionary; and Chicano activists believed Chávez to be the essence of La Causa. In fact, Chávez was all of these. His appeal varied according to the lens of perception. He did not recognize nor take advantage of his role in these terms because he was not an intellectual, a theorist, or a politician.

He was, however, what Julián Samora and the Mexican-American academics wanted: a man with a presence, rooted in the tradition and values of the Mexican community; a man who did not engage in power struggles with other Mexican-American groups nor with other Chicano leaders—Gutiérrez, Tijerina, and Gonzales. Most Mexicans and many Chicano activists agreed that Chávez and the farm workers constituted a sociopolitical movement seeking social changes within democracy, but one outside the traditional structures of organizing. Above all, most Mexican Americans understood and supported Chávez's use of his central symbol, the Virgin of Guadalupe.

The urban Mexican worker identified with Chávez's simple origins and unsophisticated manner. The middle class felt that Chávez represented both their American views and desires and their Mexican soul. Unionized Mexicans felt he was one of their own, and Chávez gave credence to their perception when he said he was impressed by John L. Lewis and Walter Reuther, two of the icons of the labor movement. Both Roman Catholic clergy (drawn to the impoverished farm workers because of the papal encyclical *Rerum Novarum* on social justice) and Protestant ministers were drawn to La Causa, indicating another important Chávez strength: his ability to bridge the traditional mistrust and hostility between Roman Catholic and Protestant. Many clergy of different denominations, as well as the Catholic intelligentsia, spoke out on behalf of Chávez and against the power of agribusiness in religious publications (e.g., *Christian Century, Catholic World, Catholic Workers,* and the *National Catholic Reporter*).

As chapter 6 has shown, the American liberal intelligentsia

molded Chávez into the role of the last Jeffersonian and pushed him into prominence in their publications. This acceptance in turn further legitimated Chávez in the eyes of Mexican Americans. In many eyes, Chávez was being transformed into a Mexican-American version of Martin Luther King Jr. Chávez's associate, Nelson, endorsed this view. He wrote in 1966: "Whether César Chávez will become the Martin Luther King of the Mexican-Americans remains to be seen. While he has penned no brilliant essays like King's, he has demonstrated remarkable leadership qualities." The truth was that Chávez's strength came from his ability to listen to advice—and at the same time maintain the respect and trust of people, serving as a focal point of various perceptions and interpretations without giving complete credence to any one in particular. To the question, "What kind of a society would you like to see in this country?" Chávez replied in an interview that he did not advocate a particular organization or ideology but felt that "so long as the smaller groups do not have the same rights and the same protection as others—I don't care whether you call it Capitalism or Communism—it is not going to work. Somehow, the guys in power have to be reached by counterpower, or through a change in their hearts and minds"—an answer that appealed to all but the most militant.

Each person could interpret Chávez's statement according to individual views, or at least believe that Chávez was not against him or her. Chávez's central strength was his strong belief that he was right in his commitment to fight for justice. He believed that all he had to do was to create an "oppositional force" for good and, as a result, people would have to respond. Matt Meier and Feliciano Rivera in their *Readings on La Raza: The Twentieth Century* believed that Chávez was often viewed as either "a Messiah or a Devil" because of his almost dogmatic belief in his "sense of righteousness." Many militant Chicanos, following Malcolm X's Islamic dictum, "The enemy of your enemy is your friend," supported Chávez. He seemed to be a metaphor for their lost Eden, their lost Aztlan.

CHÁVEZ AS "THE FIRE IN THE SOUL"

The events, ideas, criticism, and direction of the Chávez movement were carried in the pages of the UFW's well-structured,
propagandistic paper, *El Malcriado,* which reached right into
Mexican-American hearts and minds. Intellectuals such as
Acuña, the chronicler and activist, through his historical writings proposed that Chávez was the leading Chicano movement leader.

Acuña framed Chávez against a background of increasing
youth radicalization in Mexican-American communities. He
explored the Chicano themes of resistance, rebellion, anti-
colonialism, and struggle against oppression. Acuña and other
Chicano intellectuals (Carlos Muñoz, Mario Barrera, Thomas
Almaguer) saw Chávez as a leading exponent of Chicano com-
munalism, pride, identity, struggle for freedom, and a return
to the land. Chávez never contradicted, debated, or differed
with this discourse: to do so would have lost support.

Also prominent in promoting Chávez as a leader of the
radical Chicano movement were Matt Meier and Feliciano
Rivera, who in their 1969 text (still used in many Chicano
studies courses) made Chávez equal in stature to the other
radical leaders of the Chicano movement. Carlos Muñoz, a
strong supporter of Chávez in the 1960s, was one of the founders of Chicano studies programs in California and of the National Association of Chicano Studies (NACS). He was also a
leading promoter of MECHA, the major student organization. In the 1990s, as a University of California professor,
Muñoz reinterpreted Chávez and acknowledged Chávez's influence on his own politics and those of his contemporaries.
But Muñoz made clear that he did not consider Chávez to be
the leader of a *Chicano* movement:

> Chávez has been and remains the leader of a labor movement and
> later a union struggle that was never an integral part of the Chi-
> cano movement. He [Chávez] made it clear, especially during the
> movement's formative years (1968–1970), of the farm workers

union that he did not consider himself to be a Chicano leader but [simply] the organizer of a union representing a multi-racial constituency of rank-and-file workers.

Muñoz, in retrospect, was more correct than in his earlier appraisal in the 1960s. He points out in his *Youth, Identity and Power: The Chicano Movement* (1989) that Chávez never advocated nationalism. In the 1960s, rising Chicano activists, including Muñoz, simply read their own desires, goals, and ideologies into the Chávez leadership. Chicano studies academics taught (and to some extent still do teach) that Chávez was a leader of a homogenous "class" or "nationalist" movement. Just as Anglo-American radical intellectuals read U.S. history backwards, so do Chicano intellectuals. To them, every Mexican American was a Chicano; everybody who struggled was struggling for Aztlan; for the movement. And so they placed Chávez as a leader within the Chicano movement.

A leading intellectual who believed that Chávez was leader of a nationalist movement was Luis Valdez, a student-activist working for Chávez in the mid-1960s (see chapter 4). Valdez, who established the very successful El Teatro Campesino, sought to link Chávez's efforts to the rising Chicano youth movement and to the issues of identity and power. Valdez believed that the teatro united the farm workers, Chávez, and the Chicano youth to an international consciousness of struggle. The *Wall Street Journal* called Valdez's teatro "proletarian pantomine," and others, such as theater critics, Chicano intellectuals, and MECHA activists, saw El Teatro Campesino of Delano as a historical link to Aztec- Christian- Mexican- Spanish theater of fiesta, rituals, morality, and Cinco de Mayo plays and processionals. The teatro was a key to a new historical consciousness. In forging these historical and ideological links, Valdez went beyond Chávez's movement and took his actos from the *campo* to the universities and thence to the stages of Hollywood, New York, and Europe and into the movies. Although Valdez publicized Chávez's struggle and the plight of the farm workers as the "heart of Aztlan," Chávez did not feel entirely comfortable with the nationalistic and mystical ideas and directions of Valdez's teatro.

Nor did Chávez support the third-party organization of José Angel Gutiérrez's Raza Unida Party. He supported the Democratic Party and aligned himself with the Kennedys, not with militant Chicano leadership. Chávez remained steadfast in his unionism, regardless of the perceptions and aspirations others had of and for him. And yet—young Chicanos throughout the United States accepted Chávez as their own. Stan Steiner, for example, in his very popular *La Raza: The Mexican-Americans* (1969), seeking to capture the rising Chicano voices that were radicalizing Mexican-American communities, quoted one such named José, noting Chávez's influence. José, a young California radical for "Brown power," believed that Chávez was struggling for family ties and tribal ties as an alternative to the continuation of urban Los Angeles–United States culture.

Other youths, such as those involved in Corky Gonzales's Crusade for Justice in Colorado, supported Chávez because they believed that he addressed their nationalistic and antipolice ideology. They heard Chávez at a crusade rally say: "For those who have never suffered from police brutality, it is impossible to discuss the problem, and for those who have, nothing is more degrading and barbarous than police brutality. We must draw the lines once and for all." Young people in the barrios and the universities interpreted these statements within the context of a struggle against the police, the authority of the state, and a struggle for Chicano culture.

Others saw Chávez in the tradition of a Mexican peasant-revolutionary—a Zapata or a Villa. The Mexican radical tradition was the implied theme in the *Corrido of César Chávez,* an epic that lifted Chávez to the stature of a mythical folk hero:

> César walked from Delano Taking with him his faith
> Long live César Chávez And all who follow him
> Long live César Chávez
> And the Virgin [de Guadalupe] who guides him

Listen Señor César Chávez Your name is honored
On the breast you wear The Virgin de Guadalupe

Unfortunately, such songs caused many growers to feel that the Chávez movement was racial and separatist—and in fact, many young Chicanos held a similar view—though for very different reasons. To Chicano youth, Chávez was for La Raza—the people, the race. It took only a short leap of faith for barrio youth radicals, university students, and nascent Chicano intellectuals to believe that Chávez stood for separation, Third World nationalism, and class struggle. It was also only a small piece of historical fiction to make Chávez traditional heir to the Chicano struggle since the 1848 war with Mexico.

Chávez himself, in spite of the lens through which Chicano radicals perceived him, said: "La Raza? Why be racist. Our belief is to help everyone, not just one race. Humanity is our belief." Steiner wrote that when Chávez made this statement to Chicanos, "their faces fell" in disbelief.

For Chávez, civil rights was linked to a fight for human rights. He would often say of Mexican Americans, specifically the farm workers: "We are weak. And the weak have no rights, but [only] the right to sacrifice until they are strong." Young Chicanos had a somewhat different view of civil rights. Through the voice of their radical journals they argued that they wanted "the guarantee of our constitutional rights," but they felt that this meant "our rights as a people who have their own culture, their own language, their own heritage, and their own way of life." They felt and thought that Chávez, in his philosophy, meant the same thing. Chávez, meanwhile, was thinking of rights under the Declaration of Independence and the Bill of Rights.

For youths in the barrios and universities, Chávez's civil rights were cultural rights, the rights of a colonized people to self-determination, self-empowerment, and communal defense. Stan Steiner pointed out that somewhere in the Chicano mind, "civil rights became cultural rights." Consequently, for the

Chicanos of the 1960s, "Huelga! Huelga! Huelga!" and "Viva Chávez!" carried the whisper of a militant historical-cultural memory, a rhythm of political struggle, a sense of national pride, and a movement of radical activism.

Luis Valdez understood the significance of Chávez before the Chicano movement defined itself in the *Plan de Aztlan* in 1969. He reinterpreted the words *Huelga* and *Chávez,* giving them new philosophical meanings. Valdez expressed, to some extent, what the young Chicanos, farm workers, middle-class Mexican Americans, and politicians that breakfast meeting in El Paso, Texas, had sensed: that in the presence of Chávez there was something more. That morning in El Paso, Texas, Mexican Americans saw themselves in Chávez. They felt a pride in their right *to be*—to go beyond pain and sorrow. Chávez said it best: "It is a question of suffering with some kind of hope. That's better than suffering with no hope at all." Luis Solis-Garza alluded to a similar sentiment when he wrote:

> Chávez is far from being the average Mexican. As the old Mexican dicho goes, "Tiene la lumbre por dentro," meaning literally that he has a fire inside of him. And indeed, he does have a fire inside him, but, unlike a purely physical wood-burning fire which soon burns itself out, Chávez's blaze is perpetuated by a holocaust of never-ending sparks, each symbolic of a trial or tribulation of the Mexican-American plight.

Between 1964, when the farm workers' union was born, and the first major victory in 1970, Chávez became a defined reality for Mexican Americans, young and old—a source of promise, hope, and pride. Prophetically, Steiner wrote in 1969: "Chávez is an enigma to many. He is a different man to different people." That was to prove more and more true. As to Steiner's, Nelson's, and Luis Solis-Garza's question, "Who is César Chávez?" it can be said—at least in terms of what he *did*— that he sparked a realistic yet radical belief in people and in the American dream of justice.

CHAPTER 9

The Mexican Dilemma

In many ways, unionization is going to destroy the claims that undocumented workers are a drain on our society.

BERT CORONA

FOR more than forty years, the United Farm Workers, AFL–CIO, most of that time led by César Chávez, has struggled to unionize farm workers, many of them of Mexican heritage and nationality, in California and the U.S. Southwest. Beginning with the union's militant phase (the 1965 grape boycott), a recurring issue has been the union's position on Mexican immigration. On one hand, most of the union's membership has had ties of family and heritage to Mexico. On the other, Mexican immigrants were the ones being recruited to break their strikes.

The complex and changing relationship between the United Farm Workers Union, under Chávez's political direction, and the growing issue of Mexican immigration has implications for the future of the labor movement. In developing strategies to deal with the problem of government-sanctioned strikebreakers from Mexico, Chávez and the UFW sometimes had to adopt a restrictionist stance to combat the opposing powerful alliance of business and government. After 1975 and the failure of the California Farm Labor Act to help the union in its efforts to organize workers, Chávez welcomed Mexican immigrant support, as well as seeking closer relationships with Mexican *sindicatos* (unions) and the Mexican government.

This chapter considers the international dimensions of Chávez's leadership. International developments, in particular immigration from Mexico and Latin America, has had an increasing impact on everyone in the United States. The tremendous growth in the Spanish-speaking population (and the projection that it will be of increasing demographic importance), particularly in the Western states, promises to change the social and political relations between ethnic and racial groups. In this context, the history of César Chávez's struggle with the issue of Mexican immigration is very relevant. To some extent, it reflects the traditional ambivalence within the Latino population on this issue.

MEXICAN AMERICANS AND MEXICANS

The key to understanding the evolution of the United Farm Worker's policy toward Mexican immigration is the background of its leader, César Chávez. His experience as a migrant worker and organizer over the years was the most important influence in shaping the union's policy toward immigration and Mexico. During his youth, as a migrant worker with his parents, César encountered the conditions that both Mexican immigrants and Mexican Americans shared in the fields and this firsthand experience made him different from many organizers before him. The hard life gave him a strength of character that enabled him to communicate convincingly with field workers.

As a young organizer for the CSO, Chávez first faced the issue of the abuse of Mexican immigration by growers. This was in 1958, when the CSO sent him to Oxnard to help the lemon workers organize a strike for higher wages. The growers were using braceros to take the place of local resident workers, mostly nativeborn Mexican Americans. As described earlier, César successfully challenged the collusion between growers and government that had led to abuse of the Bracero Program. In the Oxnard struggle, most of the workers who were protesting the use of bracero strikebreakers were Mexican nationals legally resident in the United States—U.S. residents, but their language of organization was Spanish and their cultural values were Mexican. In opposing the exploitation of braceros, Chávez was not being anti-Mexican, and this difference was understood by the rank and file.

This same, multinational constituency was present during the grape strike and boycott. Mexican immigrants were in key roles from the beginning. In meetings and rallies, a Mexican ambience pervaded the union, Spanish being the commonly used language. Many of the workers shared bonds of common nationality. Symbolically, the day chosen to join the grape strike was 15 September, Mexican Independence day. Banners of the Virgin of Guadalupe, the patron saint of Mexico, the Mexican flag, and other Mexican symbols became an integral part of La Causa or the farm workers' movement. Several of the original members of the Farm Workers Association were immigrants of long-term residence. An example was Antonio Orendain, the young organizer who—born in Mexico—had entered the United States as a farm worker when he was eighteen and who became an important UFW organizer on the Texas border in the late 1960s.

During the California grape strike (1965 to 1970) Chávez and union supporters often spoke about the cynical manipulation and abuse of Mexican immigrant workers by the growers and the government. From the start, however, Mexican immigrants were as much a part of the problem as they were a part of the solution.

It has been well documented in contemporary accounts: Agribusiness regularly employed Mexican immigrants as strikebreakers; and Chávez and UFW leaders complained about the "porous border" with Mexico. But many UFW supporters and members were Mexican nationals. The proportion of undocumented and documented Mexican immigrants who were active in the early UFW actions varied, ranging from more than 70 percent in the Imperial Valley, adjacent to Mexico, to less than 30 percent in strikes in Florida and northern California. Mexican immigrants, however, were the ones who could most easily convince potential strikebreakers to respect picket lines. Beginning with the grape boycott of 1965, Chávez both championed the rights of immigrants and advocated vigorous police measures to enforce labor laws. The apparent contradiction between advocating the rights of Mexican immigrants to fair treatment and yet favoring immigration restrictions led, in the 1970s, to open criticism of Chávez's position by Chicano immigrant-rights activists.

TEXAS AND THE IMMIGRANTS

In 1966, a year after the Delano strike began, Chávez intervened in Texas, where Mexican immigrants were being used by growers as strikebreakers. César sent Orendain and Eugene Nelson, a young volunteer who was the son of a wealthy California grower, to lead the UFW organizing effort. In South Texas, farmworkers earned less than a dollar an hour—little more than half the California wage. That spring, the UFW organized a march to protest the abysmal wages and degraded living conditions. They marched from the border town of Rio Grande City to Austin, a distance of 450 miles.

Mexican-American melon workers along the Rio Grande were the main supporters of the UFW. They had been on strike for several months but had failed to get a contract because of the ease with which growers could enlist strikebreakers from across the border. Taking direct action before the march began, UFW organizers and Texas melon workers (the Independent Workers Association) moved to prevent strikebreakers from crossing the bridge between Roma, Texas, and Miguel Aleman, Mexico. On 24 October 1966, a group of UFW supporters began stopping buses and cars carrying farm workers across the international bridge on their way to work in Texas. In the ensuing altercation, a local sheriff dragged a UFW organizer over the line into Mexico then apprehended him for illegal entry when he stepped back into the United States. After the organizer's detention, a dozen or so UFW supporters lay down on the international bridge and stopped all traffic for about an hour. Police arrested them for obstructing traffic and, later, a state district judge issued a temporary restraining order to prevent future blockage of the bridge. A few days later, Mexican officials arrested three UFW supporters who had closed and locked the steel gate at the center of the international bridge.

These militant actions got the attention of the press. This in turn advertised the strike and the UFW also worked with Mexican unions to gain support among the border crossers. On 13 May, the Confederación de Trabajadores Mexicanos (CTM) organized a picket on the Mexican side of the border opposite Rio Grande City to discourage Mexican holders of U.S. green cards from crossing to work as scabs. UFW organizers and members joined the Mexicans on the other side of the line.

A few weeks later, five growers from the Rio Grande area sent a telegram to Senator John Tower of Texas accusing the UFW and CTM of engaging in "an international conspiracy" and a Starr County grand jury termed the strike "un-American." Meanwhile, Texas Rangers having escorted immigrant strikebreakers to work in the fields, a federal court found that the police and county authorities had engaged in illegal activities to suppress the strike.

TAKING ON THE INS

During the early years of the grape strike and boycott, the UFW organized demonstrations against the Immigration and Naturalization Service (INS) to protest their failure to prevent growers from hiring Mexican immigrants during strikes. The UFW contended that the INS was working in cooperation with the larger growers. In turn, the INS claimed that their funding was inadequate: they could not monitor strikebreakers.

During the Giumarra grape strike in 1967, Chávez met with the western regional director of the INS, charging that the INS was in violation of Justice Department regulations prohibiting the use of green carders (people with U.S. permanent resident status) in areas where a labor dispute was in progress. Chávez told the director that Giumarra, in violation of this regulation, was recruiting green-card workers from the Calexico area and taking them by bus to Delano to break the strike. The director said the INS had no jurisdiction over the employment of workers with green cards once they were admitted to the United States: the regulation required only that the INS monitor the place of employment at the time of application. He admitted, however, that there might be a technical violation of the labor laws if growers had recruited workers specifically to break a strike. Not satisfied with this response, Chávez picketed in front of the INS headquarters and organized a letter-writing campaign to pressure officials in Washington.

Controversy over green-card abuses lasted well into the next year, the Justice Department eventually ruling in favor of the growers. But Chávez and the UFW continued to protest the government's progrower policies. When Attorney General Ramsey Clark arrived in San Francisco on 29 May 1968 to speak before the National Conference of Social Welfare, the UFW met him with more than three hundred demonstrators, disrupting his speech.

The problem of government-sanctioned strikebreakers from Mexico was a serious one for the UFW. César consistently argued that in order to raise wages and to improve working conditions for all farm workers, the government needed to enforce existing laws and enact more stringent regulations. In his testimony in Washington, D.C., before the Subcommittee on Labor of the Senate Committee on Labor and Public Welfare in the late 1960s, Chávez called for employer sanctions, fines against growers who employed illegal Mexican immigrants, and penalties against green-card workers who accepted employment on a struck ranch. He told the committee, "What we ask is some way to keep the illegal and green carders from breaking our strikes; some civil remedy against growers who employ behind our picket lines those who have entered the United States illegally, and likewise those green carders who have not permanently moved their residence and domicile to the United States."

If Chávez's position sounded like that of a nativist, it was because he had to speak about the widespread grower violation of immigration laws. In June 1974, at the beginning of the grape harvest, Chávez told reporters that the union had "documented more than 2,200 illegal aliens working on ranches in the Fresno area." Chávez accused the Nixon administration of conspiring with agribusiness "to make sure this flood of desperately poor workers continued unchecked." He again accused the border patrol of working with the growers, and he demanded that the government increase its enforcement efforts. Protests against the INS and their selective enforcement of the immigration laws went on throughout the summer of 1974. In August, the UFW sponsored a demonstration in front of and inside the United States Federal Building in Sacramento, California, where 350 supporters gathered to support Assembly Bill 3370 providing for state regulation of farm-worker elections. They also protested government-grower collusion to violate the immigration laws.

Chávez and the UFW's support for hard-line enforcement measures and tough new immigration proposals (such as those proposed by Congressman Peter Rodino in 1973) led to conflict with immigration-rights activists. In July 1974, the National Coalition for Fair Immigration Laws and Practices, an alliance of Chicano and Mexican-American groups, openly criticized Chávez for his support of strict policing of the border. Later that year, when the Justice Department announced its intention to begin a massive deportation drive of illegal aliens (with the apparent blessings of the UFW leadership), a broad spectrum of Mexican-American groups attacked the government and the UFW's position. Chávez wrote an open letter to the *San Francisco Examiner*, expressing his union's position on immigration. He denied supporting the government's plan to deport millions of immigrants and again blamed the INS for allowing growers to import undocumented immigrant strikebreakers. He reiterated his concern for the exploitation of undocumented workers and promised to support an amnesty that would lead to their legalization and right to organize. This position was consistent with his views of five years earlier: that the real criminals were the growers, who violated the immigration laws. The immigrants, he maintained, were pawns in the growers' struggle with the union. This statement made public his concern for the rights of undocumented immigrants. The UFW was on record in support of undocumented immigrant rights, making special efforts to include them within the union.

THE UFW AND MEXICAN WORKERS

During the 1960s and 1970s, the UFW developed several strategies to combat the progrower policies of the border patrol and immigration service. One was to work more closely with Mexican sindicatos. Whenever the UFW organized a strike in the Imperial Valley, it inevitably came into contact with large numbers of workers from Mexicali who daily crossed the border to work in the United States. As mentioned earlier, in 1968 César asked organizer Bert Corona to go to the Imperial Valley and convince Mexican commuter workers not to break the current strike. On César's recommendation, Corona met with the president of the Mexican local of the Confederación de Trabajadores Mexicanos in Mexicali. Corona recalled: "He [the Mexican labor leader] introduced me to other Mexican labor leaders with whom we had an opportunity to talk and ask for their support." Corona obtained permission to distribute leaflets on the Mexican side, informing workers of the strike. He also got permission to place ads and stories in the Mexicali newspaper and made public service announcements on Mexicali radio and television. In an interview Corona recalled: "We were interviewed periodically and we got the message [out] about the strike through all the connections with the unions and in the communications industry. They brought pressure and they made it possible for us to carry out that work of informing and organizing."

In another case, when the cooperative, binational strategy failed, Chávez authorized more direct action. In 1974 frustrations over immigrant strikebreakers had reached a high point and some members of the UFW pushed to become more involved in enforcing the immigration laws along the border. In September, during an UFW strike of citrus pickers in Yuma, Arizona, César sent his cousin Manuel to lead the organizational efforts there. The growers, as usual, began recruiting undocumented Mexican workers from across the border. The UFW protested the inactivity of the INS and then began stopping undocumented Mexican workers at the border, trying to convince them not to scab. A predictable scenario followed: the local federal court issued orders restricting the numbers on the picket line; and confrontations between union supporters and illegal immigrants took place. Complicating the issue, many of the UFW members on strike were Mexican immigrants, some of them undocumented. This made the Yuma strike not only a struggle between the UFW and the grower/police/judiciary alliance, it also was between Mexican immigrant members of the union and Mexican immigrants who were not UFW supporters.

The strike became more volatile when, on 16 September, the FBI arrested twenty-five UFW members in Yuma, identifying them as Mexican aliens. They were charged with trespassing and disturbing the peace during a rock-throwing incident at a labor camp. Soon after the arrests, more than two hundred UFW followers demonstrated in front of the county jail. Speakers urged the crowd to go to the nearby United States Border Patrol offices in Yuma to protest the lack of enforcement by INS agents.

Four days later, UFW officials met with national park officers at the Organ Pipe National Park on the Arizona border with Sonora, Mexico. Convinced that many undocumented

immigrants were crossing the national park, the UFW noti-
fied the park officers that they were posting a roving patrol
within the park to stop the undocumented crossings. By October, the UFW had organized a "wet line" watch along the
border to deal directly with undocumented immigrant strikebreakers. UFW patrols beat up several undocumented workers
and detained others, turning them over to the border patrol.
The newspapers reported that three hundred UFW supporters
patrolled a 125-mile stretch of the border between San Luis
and Lukeville, Arizona. The union rented a plane to fly recon-
naissance for motorized union pickets. Often, the UFW people simply stopped border-crossers and talked to them about
the strike, convincing many of them not to cross. Technically
there was nothing illegal in this. In fact, William Smitherman,
a United States attorney, visited the area to observe the wet
line and later issued an advisory that these actions were not in
violation of federal statutes. César, although not personally in
charge of Yuma organization, clearly must not have been kept
informed of events. Perhaps he placed too much trust in his
cousin Manuel's ability to handle the situation.

Back in Yuma itself, the atmosphere of violence intensified.
In early October, persons unknown firebombed a labor contractor's bus and five cars owned by undocumented immigrants. A few days later the police arrested a UFW member for
carrying a concealed weapon while picketing in front of the
Bow and Arrow, a motel that catered to labor contractors and
undocumented strikebreakers. Because the violence involved
Mexican nationals, the Yuma strike raised sensitive international issues. U.S. President Gerald Ford was already scheduled to meet with Mexican President Luis Echeverria on
21 October to discuss other problems.

The violence during the Yuma strike did not signal a change
in Chávez's tactics for dealing with Mexican immigrants; rather
it seemed that some UFW organizers and supporters had strayed
from the nonviolent philosophy Chávez advocated. The strike
generated unfavorable publicity for the union, embarrassed

Chávez, did not produce any gains for the UFW, and probably hurt its recruitment efforts among Mexican nationals. The following year, the UFW deemphasized strikes as a tactic, relying more on California's new Agricultural Labor Relations Act. Yuma seemed to prove that an overtly antiimmigrant stance would not succeed.

Over the years, the UFW made it easier for Mexican workers to be part of the union. A new UFW constitution, in 1973, reflected the binational character of the union and provided the structure to give direct assistance to Mexican immigrant workers. As mentioned earlier, the constitution did not distinguish between citizens and noncitizens: it defined the union's purpose as being "to unite under its banner all individuals employed as agricultural laborers, regardless of race, creed, sex or nationality." The constitution provided for a bill of rights for all members, regardless of citizenship or legal status in the United States. Chávez thereafter made special efforts to provide union services to members residing in Mexico. In the 1980s, the UFW opened several clinics and information offices across the border for members who worked in California but lived in Mexicali or Tijuana. In addition, the union opened campesino centers, providing a variety of services to farm workers regardless of union affiliation. By 1990 there were twenty-four centers in California, two in Arizona, and one in Mexicali. These UFW service centers helped workers with their eligibility for federal-state benefits (workmen's compensation, unemployment insurance, food stamps, aid to families with dependent children, and so forth). The centers assisted Spanish-speaking workers in negotiating the federal and state bureaucracies, providing free legal counsel and translation services. For Chávez, these centers were a natural extension of the help already available to members who were United States citizens.

This section on Mexican immigrants would be incomplete without mentioning that immigrants in the union provided some of the first UFW martyrs. We recounted earlier that in

1973 a Teamsters strikebreaker shot and killed Juan de la Cruz, a sixty-year-old Mexican-born UFW veteran. Six years later, a grower killed Rufino Contreras, a UFW farm worker from Mexicali. To honor these Mexican workers, the union established two funds: the Juan de la Cruz Farm Worker's Pension Fund and the Rufino Contreras Political Action Fund.

Thus, by the end of the 1970s, Chávez and the UFW clearly supported Mexican farm workers. Unlike many of the union's critics, Chávez had to live in a world where people's livelihoods depended on preventing an unrestricted flow of immigrant labor. Consequently, he continued to support strict immigration controls.

IMMIGRATION REFORM AND INTERNATIONALIZATION

During the 1980s, Chávez and the UFW came to support immigration reform as well as proposals to strengthen the union's ties with the Mexican sindicatos and the Mexican government. With other union officials, Chávez backed proposals that resulted in Congress drafting a new immigration law, the 1986 Immigration Reform and Control Act (IRCA). This law incorporated some of the proposals that Chávez had advocated for twenty years (e.g., employer sanctions and strengthened border patrol enforcement). Chicano activists roundly criticized this law, saying it was discriminatory and a militarization of the border, but Chávez argued that the reforms would benefit the undocumented immigrant's ability to unionize and improve working conditions. He believed that legal workers would be more likely to join unions. Like other union leaders, he favored the enforcement provisions in the law because they committed the government to implementing the labor laws.

Chávez thought the IRCA both benefited those immigrant farm workers who were able to meet the amnesty provisions and would, later, benefit the UFW when immigrant workers grew dissatisfied with pre-IRCA wages and working conditions. Over time, he figured, a revolution of rising expectations would result. The newly legalized farm workers would organize to solidify their position within American society:

> I think they'll always support, if not our union, the idea of a union [he said]. The better wages they have, the better support we have for the union. The worse the wages, the worse conditions, the harder it is to get them. When a work force is not afraid, it bargains for itself. They have a lot at stake in their families, because they are trying to get a house. They're fed up with the camp. They want their own home. Their needs are greater.

Nevertheless, the new law held potential to hurt the union. A section of the legislation, which Chávez and the UFW opposed, enabled agribusiness to import contract laborers in the event of a certified labor shortage. In essence, this provision created a program not unlike the Bracero Program. IRCA did make it easier for the UFW to recruit members. The amnesty provisions of the law, in particular those legalizing temporary agricultural workers, increased the mobility and self-confidence of a large segment of farm workers. IRCA increased the value of ties between the UFW and Mexican organizations since the increased number of legal Mexican nationals within the UFW created a new dynamic. This dynamic led to a more formal and public international policy toward Mexico. Chávez traveled to Mexico several times to discuss labor issues with a series of Mexican presidents and high-level labor officials. The union also held press conferences to protest the mistreatment of Mexican nationals by the INS and other United States authorities.

In other international developments, in the late 1980s Chávez publicly complained about the corruption in the Mexican postal system that resulted in the theft of remittances—money sent by workers to families in Mexico. He then lobbied the Mexican legislature to promote new laws to make the postal service more secure. In addition, in 1990 UFW representatives successfully lobbied Mexican legislators to pass a bill that would allow families of UFW members resident in the United States to qualify for Mexican social security benefits. On 23 April,

Chávez met with President Salinas de Gortari in Los Angeles and signed an agreement with the Mexican Social Security administration. News of this historic pact between the Mexican government and an American labor union appeared in most of Mexico's major newspapers and magazines; but it was largely ignored by the United States press. The compact undoubtedly made the UFW attractive to Mexican immigrants. In addition to its provisions, the agreement illustrated the high regard in which the Mexican government held Chávez and the UFW. In 1991, Mexico awarded Chávez the prestigious Aguila de Oro, an award of merit given to few who are not Mexican citizens. The honor recognized his contributions to the welfare of hundreds of thousands of Mexican workers in the United States. The following year, the National Autonomous University of Mexico honored Chávez with the award of el Premio Benito Juárez. This award, annual since 1988, honors an individual of international importance who has advanced the cause of justice and peace.

A BINATIONAL LABOR ORGANIZATION

Evaluations of Chávez's and the UFW's attitudes toward Mexican immigration have differed widely. For some, Chávez has simply responded to political pressures. Chicano historian David Gutiérrez, finding that, during the mid 1970s, Mexican-American organizations and leaders made a "fundamental realignment" on the issue of Mexican immigration, says they united for the first time against restrictionist immigration proposals and discovered a common interest between immigrants and nativeborn Mexican Americans—and pressured Chávez into softening his position on immigration control.

During the 1980s, Chávez joined with leaders of other organizations (such as the American G.I. Forum and the League of United Latin American Citizens) to denounce deportation plans of undocumented immigrants. Since the 1960s, Chávez had supported the human rights of Mexican immigrants, whether documented or not. The nature of this support was mainly to protest the exploitation of immigrant workers by the growers. In the seventies, along with other activists Chávez became more outspoken about immigrant rights. In the debates over Carter administration immigration proposals, the UFW, by supporting the immigrants, was not changing its policy or orientation. Chávez emphasized his support for the legalization provisions of the proposed immigration bill; but he also approved of strict enforcement measures. This position was entirely consistent with his previous statements. The hard realities of farm-labor organizing compelled Chávez and the UFW to support immigration restrictions that were not popular with Chicano activists. At the same time, the increasingly Mexican membership of the UFW encouraged the union to forge alliances with Mexican unions and Mexican government officials.

But Chávez himself changed. During his thirty years of labor organizing, he moved from a nativist stance toward Mexican immigration to a more internationalist approach. Mexican immigration shaped the UFW to become one of the few binational unions in the United States. In Mexico, writers and politicians have shown more interest in the U.S. Chicano political movement and, as a result, the farm workers' union and Chávez have become part of the folklore of the Mexican struggle against United States hegemony. President Salinas de Gortari's initiatives to forge links with Mexican-American leaders heightened the importance of César Chávez and the UFW in the views of Mexican policymakers.

The UFW has always had a sizable contingent of immigrants, documented and undocumented, in its rank and file. Since the amnesty provisions of the IRCA law of 1986, more UFW members have become legal residents. The number of recently "amnestied" workers among new members is not documented. Despite the restrictions enacted by the IRCA, the indications are that the Mexican immigrant flow is not lessening. But these new workers are no longer a threat to UFW strikes. The dilemmas posed by the failure of the California ALRB and continued Mexican immigration gave additional urgency to the UFW's grape boycott. By 1990 Chávez had an additional challenge to face: a proposed Free Trade Agreement between the United States and Mexico. If enacted, the lowering of trade barriers promised to have a negative effect on labor in the United States. The importation of agricultural goods from Mexico might create additional unemployment of farm workers in the United States and the net result would be detrimental to all United States resident farm workers, those within and without the UFW.

CHAPTER 10

Conclusion: A Legacy of Struggle

IN the early 1990s, César Chávez continued his fight for the farm workers. It was period of tremendous struggle and sacrifice. Journalists and op-ed writers occasionally devoted space to the problems the union faced, and the media's mood was largely pessimistic, if not critical. Essayists again blamed the declining fortunes of the UFW on the contradictory nature of César's leadership. His advocacy of democracy in union organization was contrasted with the increasing role of the Chávez family in top positions. Another anomaly seemed to be his trust in volunteer workers alongside his efforts to professionalize the union's administration. His loyalty to old friends and allies was undermined by bitter attacks by liberal journalists—enthusiastic supporters from the 1970s—who now were more critical. They reported internal dissent in the union. These criticisms hurt Chávez and forced him to draw to him a tight circle of loyalists.

The union was also beset with serious financial problems, arising from lawsuits. In 1991, the 4th District Court in California upheld an earlier judgment against the UFW, in favor of Daggio Inc., an Imperial Valley grower, for $1.7 million (and including interest, the final cost to the union could exceed $2.4 million). The award arose out of a 1979 strike by vegetable workers that resulted in property damage and the death of striker Rufino Contreras. To pay the fine, the UFW mounted a nationwide direct-mail campaign. But almost immediately another lawsuit threatened the UFW's existence, this one by Bruce Church Inc., who won a $5.4 million judgment for damages alleged to have been incurred during the boycott. The union appealed and is still waiting for a final resolution.

Chávez continued to appear at fund-raising rallies at college and university campuses and traveled to promote the grape boycott. He also stepped up organizing in the fields. Ranch by ranch and week by week during the summer and fall of 1992, César and the UFW staff sought to advance the union's issues. He continued organizing the grape boycott to force growers to sign contracts controlling pesticide use. In 1992, the union helped organize large-scale walkouts in the Coachella Valley during the summer grape harvest, protesting a lack of drinking water and sanitary facilities. They won concessions from the grower, allowing a workers' committee to watchdog the situation. Also in 1992, in the San Joaquin Valley, Chávez organized walkouts and protests; and in the Salinas Valley, more than ten thousand farm workers, led by Chávez, staged a protest march in support of better conditions in the fields.

Up to his death, Chávez remained confident about the ultimate success of the UFW. In late April 1993 he traveled to San Luis, Arizona (near his birthplace), to testify in the union's appeal against the $5.4 million award to Bruce Church Inc. Chávez stayed with a farm worker family and early in the week began a fast to gain moral strength. On Thursday his friends convinced him to break his fast and he went to sleep, apparently exhausted. That night, he died in his sleep.

The unexpected death of Chávez on 23 April 1993 was a major shock to his supporters throughout the world. The outpouring of condolences that followed was testimony to his importance: he was a leader who had touched the conscience of America. In addition to President Clinton's "authentic hero" proclamation, Art Torres, a state senator, for example, called him "our Ghandi" and "our Dr. Martin Luther King." Lane Kirkland, president of the AFL-CIO, said that "the improved lives of millions of farm workers and their families will endure as a testimonial to César and his life's work."

Field workers, too, offered eulogies: Manuel Amaya said: "God has taken the strongest arm that we have, but we will continue." Remigio Gutiérrez said: "For all the workers, César was strong." But César himself had perhaps given the best eulogy, nine years earlier. Speaking before the Commonwealth Club of San Francisco, in 1984, he said: "Regardless of what the future holds for our union, regardless of what the future holds for farm workers, our accomplishments cannot be undone. The consciousness and pride that were raised by our union are alive and thriving inside millions of young Hispanics who will never work on a farm."

On the day of the funeral—Thursday, 29 April—more than 35,000 people followed the casket for three miles, from downtown Delano to the union's old headquarters at Forty Acres. They came from Toronto, Miami, Mexico . . . but mostly from California, where Chávez had worked most of his life. Parents took their children out of school and drove all night to give them the experience of participating in the funeral of a great leader of the poor. Middle-class Chicanos, taking time from work, marched—some perhaps for the first time—under a UFW flag. Cardinal Roger Mahony, who had worked as a mediator for the UFW more than twenty years earlier, led the huge outdoor mass, offering a personal condolence from the pope. César's twenty-seven grandchildren went up to the altar to lay on it a carving of a UFW eagle and a short-handled hoe. Dolores Huerta delivered the eulogy for the man she had worked with for more than forty years. Luis Valdez and the Teatro Campesino paid the final tribute. "You shall never die," said Valdez, "The seed of your heart will keep on singing, keep on flowering, for the cause."

REMEMBERING CHÁVEZ

Not often does it occur that one must consciously participate in a historical event. The authors of this book did so, that Thursday, with the thousands marching in Delano in honor of

The last march, 29 April 1993. Mourners follow the casket of César Chávez through Delano during a three-mile funeral procession. Mourners, including Representative Joseph Kennedy, son of the late Robert Kennedy (left foreground), accompany the casket onto Forty Acres, the site of the UFW field office complex. Photo: *San Diego Union-Tribune*/Don Kohlbauer.

the memory of César Chávez. We were not quite sure what to expect, but we knew that we had to go.

We both had met and supported Chávez and the union in the late 1960s. Consequently, personal memories, personal reflections, and the fact that we had just finished jointly writing a biography of Chávez drove us—willingly—to pay our last respects. We certainly knew that many people would be there, but we were not prepared for the 35,000 and more that marched and went to the requiem mass.

Many were there to remember personal or public experiences of Chávez; many to experience "the end of an era." Some were there to liberate, to resurrect César Chávez from being merely a union leader, a Mexican-American hero, or a Chicano symbol. Many had already started to see him as a national metaphor of justice, humanity, equality, and freedom. It seemed that many of us were there, consciously or not, to place César Chávez in the pantheon of national and international American heroes—a tribute underscored by the statements sent by the pope, the president of Mexico, and President Clinton.

Most of the marchers were farm workers and their families: they had been touched by Chávez's presence. Also, many old students, old activists, now turned academics and intellectuals, were there to feel the innocence of the sixties, the fieriness of yesteryear's rebellion, the *lumbre* of Chávez's heart and will. We wanted that period back. Some of us had with us our children, hoping to give them an experience of continuity with our past.

The farm workers on the march felt Chávez in their hearts. We, the professors, felt him also in our heads—we were there to interpret. We were there along with the Chicano artists Montoya, Olmos, Alurista and others: in part to recall the romance that we once had with Chávez. However, if we could not feel it, we could at least write about it, or teach it. For us all, Chávez was the soul we had partly lost, not necessarily our ethnic one, nor our political one, but our human soul. Chávez, throughout his more than thirty years of organizing, never lost his spirit; he never became totally partisan in his politics. He believed in everyone—regardless of race or color. For Chávez, everyone was equal and deserved respect, dignity, and love.

Chávez always believed the words that thousands chanted on the march: *Se puede; si se puede*—It can be done, yes it can be done. Marching, we remembered Chávez's determination and constant hope; his deep belief that people can accomplish the impossible with cooperation, and God's help, as well as with hard work. Before Jesse Jackson said "Keep hope alive," Chávez had urged it. Before Jackson called for a Rainbow Coalition, Chávez had formed one. Before the Kennedys discovered the liberal mystique of the poor and poverty, Chávez had lived it and embraced it. And there they were—the Kennedy clan. Jesse Jackson, Willie Brown, Ron Dellums, Jerry Brown, Edward James Olmos, Jimmy Smits, Cheech Marin, Paul Rodriguez, Luis Valdez, the members of El Teatro Campesino, the Culture Clash comedy group, Martin Sheen, a remnant of the Brown Berets, and many other artists, politicians, and public figures. It was, in many ways, the sixties revisited. We felt the past being remade, the present suspended, and the future reenergized. It was a funeral, but it was more: it was a celebration of humanity and hope, a resurrection of Chávez's spirit: a *día de los Santos,* and a *día de los Muertos.*

For some, especially young people, it was a march of awareness, a day of learning and understanding, a forming of a new consciousness. We envied the fresh eyes from which they saw the march, the mass, the crowds, the waving flags, the priests, the politicians, the artists, and the farm workers. It was the young who, because of their perspective, allowed us to see beyond the chaos, hopelessness, and fragmentation of postmodern America. For a brief moment of time—that Thursday in 1993—on a hot day in Delano, we experienced the struggle, the life, and the tensions that Chávez had experienced: marching in the heat, thirsty, hungry, and sleepy. It was a renewal of community: we remembered; youth recognized. Briefly in Delano that hot day, we were all campesinos. We were one with César Chávez. We were part of the land, the struggle, and Chávez's hope that humanity would survive.

Together, we knew that as long as there were people like these young Chicanos/Latinos—and people who are observant, caring, romantic, and knowledgeable about the character, cause, and meaning of Chávez—there will be hope. Chávez the activist, alive and struggling in the 1960s, we once thought was only for us: the Chicanos, the Mexican Americans, the *Americans,* the radicals, the liberals, the innocent, the romantic—the ones who cared and were striving for a more just and equitable society. But now, in death, Chávez could be for everyone—all the new Hispanic and American generations of the 1990s and beyond, the generations of the twenty-first century. He could be a guiding mentor like Dr. Martin Luther King Jr. or John F. Kennedy. In a world in need of heroes, he (and people like Dolores Huerta) could be remembered for justice, freedom, and the hope of a new humanity. Chávez said almost thirty years ago:

> I am convinced that the truest act of courage, the strongest act of humanity, is to sacrifice ourselves for others in a totally non-violent struggle for justice . . . to be human is to suffer for others. . . . God help us to be human.

These words were given to us by the Chávez family in the program for the day. As the day ended, Chávez became for us, not a text that we had just written, but an authentic friend again.

Bibliographical Essay

MORE has been written about César Chávez than about any other person of Mexican descent in the history of the United States. A student will soon discover that it is impossible to separate the story of César Chávez, the man, from the story of La Causa, the farm workers' movement. Despite a considerable body of secondary literature and a sizable public archive located at Wayne State University, a definitive biography will have to wait: historians are still too close to the events to be able to construct a balanced account. César's life has been so involved with the politics of the farm-labor movement that, at this point, it is difficult to gain access to the documents and persons who could tell the whole story. The two sides of the labor struggle are still polarized by decades of strife. César remains a controversial figure in U.S. history and his life story is part of a continuing political struggle that makes objectivity difficult.

This book has sought to interpret the life and work of César Chávez in terms of those historical forces by which he was surrounded, the emergence of the Chicano movement, the lingering heyday of New Deal–type of liberals, and the shaping influence on the farm-labor union of women like Dolores Huerta. We do not see him primarily as a labor leader, a reformer, a spiritual teacher, a Chicano activist, or a tragic hero. We see him as all of these things combined—an indefinable essence. In this sense we feel that we have contributed a new perspective on César Chávez. Of course, we have relied a great deal on the work of many other scholars, to whom we are indebted. The bibliographic discussion below indicates those works we feel are among the most important—books, articles, and scholarly dissertations on the man and his work. The secondary works we have referenced in our text, apart from those cited previously, are Rudolfo Acuña, *Occupied America: A History of Chicanos,* 3d ed. (New York: Prentice Hall, 1987), Matt S. Meier and Feliciano Rivera, *The Chicanos: A History of Mexican Americans* (New York: Hill and Wang, 1972), and Stan Steiner, *La Raza: The*

Mexican Americans (New York: Harper, 1970). Compilations of essays about Chávez and the UFW which give a picture of the man as viewed by his contemporaries are by Julian Samora, ed., *La Raza: Forgotten Americans* (Notre Dame: University of Notre Dame Press, 1966), Edward Simmen, ed., *Pain and Promise: The Chicano Today* (New York: New American Library, 1972), Meier and Rivera, eds., *Readings on La Raza, The Twentieth Century* (New York: Hill and Wang, 1974), and Manuel P. Servin, comp., *An Awakened Minority: the Mexican Americans* (Beverly Hills: Glencoe Press, 1974). Other works that give a more contemporary interpretation are Carlos Muñoz, Jr., *Youth Identity, Power: The Chicano Movement* (London and New York: Verso Press, 1989), and Richard Rodriguez, *Days of Obligation: An Argument with My Mexican Father* (New York: Viking, 1992).

THE FIRST TEN YEARS

The first ten years of the UFW movement (1965–1975) are well documented. Jacques E. Levy's book, *César Chávez: Autobiography of La Causa* (New York: W. W. Norton, 1975) is recognized as the best account of César's life up to about 1974. Unabashedly pro-union and pro-Chávez, Levy's book is a collection of transcribed oral reminiscences by Chávez and other union organizers and supporters over a period of years. Levy was given access to the inner circle of advisers around Chávez from 1969 to 1975, and he was present at many of the events described in the oral interviews. The procedure Levy used was peripatetic. He traveled with César as he went around the country and collected his remembrances on the run. Later he read the transcribed interviews back to Chávez to check for accuracy and to edit. Levy captured very intimate moments as César remembered his childhood in Arizona and the hard times his family endured as migrants in the San Joaquin Valley. Levy also collected the impressions of the people closest to Chávez—his wife Helen, Dolores Huerta, and relatives. The Levy book (which we have quoted on pages 5–7, 12, 15, 17, 25, 27, 30, 33, 37–38, 46–48, 51, 60, 78, 84–88, 108–111, and 115) is unsurpassed as a primary source.

Levy's book is the most comprehensive source produced by union insiders. In this category also are books by Eugene Nelson, *Huelga: The First Hundred Days of the Great Delano Grape Strike* (Delano: Farm Workers Press, 1966), and Mark Day, *Forty Acres: César Chávez and the Farm Workers* (New York: Praeger Publishers, 1971). Nelson, son of a Delano grower, was converted to the UFW cause early in 1965. Later, César put him in charge of organizing UFW activities in South Texas. His book, a journalistic narrative, tells (as the title suggests) of the events at the beginning of the grape strike in Delano. Especially valuable are his reports of what was said at union meetings and rallies. Day's book is that of a priest who worked with Chávez between 1968 and 1971. Originally from Stockton, Day was editor of the union's newspaper, *El Malcriado*. In addition to including a brief account of César's background, this book covers the three years during Day's stint as a volunteer. *Forty Acres* is mostly a series of firsthand accounts of the grape strike and boycott, the negotiations with the growers, personal glimpses of Chávez and others around him, and comments on the role of the church in the strike.

Other biographical sources are the journalistic portraits written by liberals caught up with drama of the struggle. A number of newspapers and magazines began to cover the union and Chávez in 1966. The first major national coverage was an extensive interview with Chávez, "An Organizers Tale," that appeared in *Ramparts Magazine*, July 1966. An interview with Luis Valdez also appeared in the same issue of the magazine. Later, books by Peter Mathiessen, Jacques Levy, and Ronald Taylor would draw from these interviews.

The first book on the movement was by John Dunne, *Delano, Story of the California Grape Strike* (New York: Farrar, Straus & Giroux, 1967). Drawing on interviews and firsthand observations during the first two years of the grape strike and boycott (1965–1967), Dunne presents a report of events balancing the impressions of growers, town residents, and nonunion members with those of Chávez and UFW advocates. Chávez himself is portrayed as a hardheaded labor leader, not a saint. Dunne is critical of the self-righteousness on both sides and discusses conflicts between the Filipino and Mexican members of the UFW. Dunne's account ends with the Sierra Vista elections in 1967.

Peter Matthiessen's *Sal Si Puedes: César Chávez and the New American Revolution* (New York: Random House, 1969) is a less critical interpretation of the early years. Originally written as a series to appear in the *New Yorker* (21 and 28 June 1969), Matthiessen's literary account gives a vivid narrative of Chávez's early life and of the grape strike. The book is an expanded version of the articles. Matthiessen added more historical background and personal reflections to the original text and succeeded, as few other nonunion interviewers have, in getting close to Chávez's family. The result is a sympathetic picture of César as a multidimensional person.

In 1975, two more journalistic biographies of Chávez and *el movimiento* appeared, one authored by Ronald Taylor, *Chávez and the Farm Workers* (Boston: Beacon, 1975), and another by Sam Kushner,

The Long Road to Delano (New York: International Publishers, 1975). These were both books by liberal journalists, one from California (Taylor) and the other from New York (Kushner). Taylor was a reporter for the *Fresno Bee* and his day-to-day involvement with farm politics in the San Joaquin Valley led to a realistic, sympathetic portrait of Chávez. Taylor's book, full of material gathered over many years of interviews with growers, government officials, and Chávez and others in the union is perhaps the best biography we have read on Chávez (we are categorizing Levy's book as an autobiography). Taylor supplies a wealth of detail about Chávez's life not found in any other source. His story is written with an eye to journalistic objectivity, a balance largely missing in Kushner's account. Taylor's book is tightly written and includes information based on original interviews with Chávez and his supporters. This book is the only one of the studies of Chávez to be reprinted in translation in Mexico, *Chávez, la interminable batalla por la dignidad* (Mexico, D.F.: Edamex, 1979).

Kushner, a seasoned labor union activist, interpreted Chávez's life and times in light of the history of farm labor in California. The book contains much historical background and includes a strongly pro-union interpretation. As a veteran trade unionist, Kushner furnishes inside anecdotes of the tactics and views of the union officials in the AFL-CIO, UAW, ILWU, and Teamsters. His is a rambling book, full of information about labor politics, past and present.

Another sympathetic record of Chávez and the UFW is Paul Fusco and George D. Horowitz, *La Causa: The California Grape Strike* (New York: Collier, 1970). Then there is Joan London and Henry Anderson, *So Shall Ye Reap* (New York: Thomas Crowell, 1970), and Jan Young, *The Migrant Workers and César Chávez* (New York: Julian Messner, 1972). All these books emphasize the farm-labor movement and Chávez's leadership. Of another kind is the scholarly study by Winthrop Yinger, *César Chávez: The Rhetoric of Nonviolence* (Hicksville, N.Y.: Exposition, 1975), which is a study of the content of several Chávez speeches.

LA CAUSA IN THE 1970S AND 1980S

Following the publication of the books by Levy, Taylor, and Kushner, other major books about Chávez appeared in the late 1970s and early 1980s: Dick Meister and Anne Loftis, *A Long Time Coming: The Struggle to Unionize America's Farm Workers* (New York: Macmillan, 1977), gives a standard overview of Chávez's early struggles and brings the story up to date (1977) with accounts of the battles to establish the Agricultural Labor Relations Board (ALRB), negotiations with Jerry Brown, and the union's protests over the ALRB process.

Craig J. Jenkins, *The Politics of Insurgency: The Farm Workers Movement in the 1960s* (New York: Columbia University Press, 1985) is the first book on Chávez published by a university press. It is a well-written analysis of the UFW and Chávez's leadership up to 1980. Jenkins emphasizes the twists and turns in union strategies and discusses theories of insurgency and mobilization in relation to farm-labor history.

Sydney D. Smith, *Grapes of Conflict* (Pasadena, California: Hope, 1987) tells the story of the California Migrant Ministry's involvement in supporting the grape strike and the UFW. Smith was in the migrant ministry along with two UFW advisors, Jim Drake and Chris Hartmire. His account focuses mainly on the ministry's organization; only secondarily on Chávez.

Fred Ross, Chávez's mentor, has written his recollections of César's early days working with the Community Service Organization (CSO). *Conquering Goliath: César Chávez at the Beginning* (Keene, California: Taller Grafico, 1989) is full of direct quotes of remembered meetings and conversations and tells the story from Ross's point of view. It is one of the few books about Chávez to have his personal endorsement and that of the union. A biography of Philip Vera Cruz, an early cofounder of the UFW, is by Craig Scharlin and Lilia V. Villanueva, *Philip Vera Cruz: A Personal History of Filipino Immigrants and the Farm Workers Movement* (Los Angeles: UCLA Institute of Industrial Relations and UCLA Asian American Studies Center, 1992).

Several excellent article-length studies about Chávez, Dolores Huerta, and the UFW have been published. Barbara L. Baer and Glenna Matthews, "The Women of the Boycott," in the *The Nation* (218, 23 February 1974: 232–238) was perhaps the first major attempt to recognize the importance of Dolores Huerta and other UFW women. Other sources containing information and interviews with Dolores Huerta are Ruth Carranza, "From the Fields into the History Books," *Intercambios Femeniles* 3 (Winter 1989); Jean Murphy, "Unsung Heroine of La Causa," *Regeneracion* 1 (1991); Luis Valdez, "Dolores Huerta: A Tribute," *San Francisco Examiner Sunday Image Magazine*, 12 August 1990; and Joan M. Jensen, *With These Hands: Women Working on the Land* (Old Westbury, New York: The McGraw Hill Book Co., 1981). The lengthy interview with Huerta is especially revealing of her personal life and philosophy. Another important study is the essay by Cletus E. Daniel, "César Chávez and the Unionization of California Farm Workers," in *Labor Leaders in America*, Melvyn Dubofsky and Warren Van Tine, eds. (Urbana and Chicago: University of Illinois Press, 1987). This essay is a thoughtful interpretation of Chávez's activism in terms of his childhood experiences and training as an organizer. Most importantly, Daniel attempts to deal with the issue of the union's decline during the 1980s, attributing it (p. 380) to "a web of complex factors related to the sometimes contradictory leadership of César Chávez" as well as to the politicized nature of the ALRB.

Until 1971, most of the published accounts of the UFW and Chávez had been sympathetic. Then more critical views of the man and the movement began to emerge, beginning with a scurrilous book by Ralph de Toledano, *Little Cesar* (New York: Anthem Press, 1971). Other critical stories appeared in Republican and pro-agribusiness journals and newspapers. Ironically, the most critical attacks came from the Left: a series of articles in the *Village Voice* by Jeff Coplon, "César Chávez's Fall from Grace," (14 and 21 August 1984). Articles in a similar vein appeared in regional journals and newspapers; (e.g., John Hubner's "The God of the Movement," in *West*, 19 August 1984).

Since Chávez's death, hundreds of articles have appeared in major news magazines and newspapers, summarizing his career and eulogizing his life. The consensus seemed to be that, despite the decline in union strength in the 1980s, Chávez was an important reformer who fought the good fight against tremendous odds. President Clinton's funeral message urged all Americans to reflect on César Chávez's legacy—a struggle for justice, a sense of compassion for the poor, and a strong commitment to moral leadership (Proclamation 6552—death of César Chávez. *Weekly Compilation of Presidential Documents* 29, no. 17 (3 May 1993:709). Peter Matthiessen reflected on Chávez's self-sacrifice and total dedication ("César Chávez," *New Yorker* 69, no. 13, 17 May 1993). All the major news magazines carried summaries of his career, emphasizing his nonviolent philosophy and dedication (David Gates, "A Secular Saint of the '60s: César Chávez, farm workers' champion, 1927–1993," *Newsweek* 121, no. 18, (3 May 1993:68); "Died, César Chávez, 66," *Time* 141, no. 18 (3 May 1993:25). Only one critical obituary appeared: Frank Bardacke "César's Ghost: Decline and Fall of the U.F.W." *Nation* 257, no. 4 (26 July 1993) blamed the decline of the UFW on the total control of Chávez and the overreliance on boycotts.

DISSERTATIONS AND THESES

Most of the academic work on Chávez has focused on specific theoretical problems dealing with the labor movement. Biographical information is usually secondary in these works. A topical listing of dissertations and theses indicates the nature of this specialized literature, some of which is valuable for biographers.

Women in the UFW

Barbara Jeane Cram, "Women Organizers in the United Farm Workers: Their Motivation and Perceptions of Sexism Within the Union." Master's thesis, CSU Fullerton, Woman's Studies, 1981.

Margaret Eleanor Rose, "Women in the United Farm Workers: A Study of Chicana and Mexicana Participation in a Labor Union." Ph.D. diss., UCLA, History, 1988.

Legal Issues

Ellen Casper, "A Social History of Farm Labor in California with Special Emphasis on the United Farm Workers Union and California Rural Legal Assistance." Ph.D. diss., New School for Social Research, Sociology, 1984.

Robert Joseph Mitchell, "Peace in the Fields: A Study of the Passage and Subsequent History of the California Agricultural Labor Relations Act of 1975." Ph.D. diss., UC Riverside, Political Science, 1980.

Theoretical Implications

Jerald Barry Brown, "The United Farm Workers Grape Strike and Boycott, 1965–1970: An Evaluation of the Culture of Poverty Theory." (Ph.D. diss., Cornell University, Anthropology, 1972).

Paul Anthony Hribar, "The Social Fasts of César Chávez: A Critical Study of Nonverbal Communication, Nonviolence, and Public Opinion." Ph.D. diss., University of Southern California, Speech, 1978).

Donovan O. Roberts, "Theory and Practice in the Life and Thought of César E. Chávez: Implications for a Social Ethic." Ph.D. diss., Boston University, Graduate School, 1979).

Jimmy Lee Shaw, "Gramsci's Theory of Hegemony and the United Farm Workers: An Empirical Case Study." Ph.D. diss., University of Kansas, Sociology, 1983).

Jane M. Yett, "Farm Labor Struggles in California 1970–73 in Light

of Reinhold Niebuhr's Concept of Power and Justice." Ph.D.
diss., Graduate Theological Union, Berkeley, 1980.

Other Dissertations and Theses

Elaine Graves, "*El Malcriado* Anthology, 1965–1972." (Master's thesis, University of Connecticut at Fairfield, 1969).
Robert M. Heisly, "Corridistas de la Huelga: Songmaking and Singing in the Lives of Two Individuals." Ph.D. diss., UCLA, Sociology, 1983).

PHOTOGRAPHIC COLLECTIONS, FILMS, AND
CHILDREN'S BOOKS

The dramatic early years of the UFW have generated thousands of
photographs by participants and journalists. Almost every author of
a book about Chávez has his or her own collection of photographs.
In addition, the union archives at Wayne State University, Detroit,
Michigan, has a hugh collection of photos.

Published books with a photographs of the early days of the grape
strike are Paul Fusco and George D. Horowitz, *La Causa: The
California Grape Strike* (New York: Collier, 1970), and George Ballis,
Basta! The Tale of Our Struggle (Delano: Farm Workers Press, 1966).
Jacques Levy also has a good selection of photographs.

The United Farm Workers union has made a number of issue-
oriented films that make appeals to the public to join the struggle.
The union has not issued a documentary devoted entirely to Chávez.
Fighting for Our Lives (1973) was filmed during the struggle with the
Teamsters and presents the UFW case dramatically, showing the
funeral of one of the farm workers killed in the struggle. *The Wrath
of Grapes* (1987) was made to generate support for a new grape
boycott, targeting the issue of pesticide use in the fields and its
consequences for the workers and consumers.

The National Education Media made *Decision at Delano* (1982),
chronicling the early days of the grape strike, and another private
producer made *The Golden Cage: A Story of California's Farm Workers*
(1990), a prizewinning history of the UFW using historical footage,
interviews, and still photographs.

Chávez's life has been the subject of a number of children's books,
the aim being to offer Chávez as a positive role model for both
young Latinos and non-Latinos. A sampling is James Terzian and
Kathryn Cramer, *Mighty Hard Road: The Story of César Chávez*
(Garden City, New York: Doubleday, 1970); Rudolf Gómez, *The*

Changing Mexican-American (El Paso: University of Texas, 1972); Roger Axford, *Spanish-Speaking Heroes* (Midland, Michigan: Pendell, 1973); Florence White, *César Chávez, Man of Courage* (Champaign, Illinois: Garrard, 1973); and Maurice Roberts, *César Chávez and La Causa* (Chicago: Children's Press: 1986).

BIBLIOGRAPHIES AND ARCHIVES

The only published bibliography of Chávez and the union is Beverly Fodell, *César Chávez and the United Farm Workers: A Selective Bibliography* (Detroit: Wayne State University, 1974). This bibliography lists many but not all of the journal and newspaper articles about Chávez. A follow-up bibliography covering the years up to 1976 and entitled *Selected Bibliography: United Farm Workers, 1973–1976* is available in typescript from the Walter Reuther Archives of Wayne State University, site of the official UFW archives. A complete listing of the archival collections pertaining to the UFW can be found in *A Guide to the Archives of Labor History and Urban Affairs: Wayne State University,* compiled and edited by Warner W. Pflug (Detroit: Wayne State University Press, 1974). The holdings of the Wayne State archives have several restrictions on them. For example, material within the last fifteen years is not available to researchers without prior authorization from the UFW and some of the their collections are closed indefinitely to the public. Those who want to get a feel for the UFW's position on the many issues involving farm workers should consult the union's newspaper, *El Malcriado,* available on microfilm from several libraries. The microfilm edition, however, stops at 1972. Since then, the paper has published occasionally and is available in a complete series only at the union's headquarters in La Paz. The UFW archives at La Paz include collections of published and unpublished materials relating to Chávez and the union. Access to this information requires prior permission from the union. Another archival source is the papers of El Teatro Campesino, held by the University of California at Santa Barbara, Chicano Studies Library, Colleccion Tlatoque.

Index

A & P, boycott of, 127
Abernathy, Ralph, 90
Access, union organizer rights of,
129, 130
Accident insurance, as strike issue, 14
Acuña, Rodolfo, 145, 147–49, 151,
179
Adams, Henry, 115
AFL. *See* American Federation of
Labor
AFL-CIO (American Federation of
Labor-Congress of Industrial
Organizations), 111, 116, 117, 123,
182; and AWOC, 32; farm work-
ers embraced by, 55 (*see also*
United Farm Workers Organiz-
ing Committee); and Schenley/
FWA contract, 53; and Team-
ster/UFW problem, 117, 126;
UFW backup from, 127. *See also*
Kircher, Bill
Agribusiness: Matthiessen on, 103;
religious publications vs., 149;
U.S. subsidization of, 140
Agricultural Labor Relations Act,
California, 128, 166
Agricultural Labor Relations Board
(ALRB), California, 129–30, 171;
establishment of, 183; grower tilt
of, 135, 184; UFW differences
with, 183
Agricultural Workers Association,
30–31
Agricultural Workers Organizing
Committee. *See* AWOC
Aguila de Oro, 169

Alabama, state of: civil rights activ-
ism in, 41
Alatorre, Richard, 128, 134
Alianza Federal de Mercedes Li-
bres, 57–58, 83–84, 139
Aliens, Mexican. *See* Immigrants,
illegal Mexican
Alinsky, Saul, 24, 60, 65, 67, 72, 112,
148
Almaguer, Thomas, 151
ALRB. *See* Agricultural Labor Re-
lations Board
Alurista (Chicano poet), 141, 176
Amaya, Manuel, 174
American Federation of Labor
(AFL), 16. *See also* AFL-CIO
American Federation of Labor–
Congress of Industrial Organiza-
tions. *See* AFL-CIO
American G.I. Forum, 27, 143, 169
Amnesty, as IRCA feature, 167, 168,
170
Anderson, Henry, 112–14
Anglos: Chávez respect for, 145;
Chávez supporters among, 51, 56,
139
Anticommunism: as Alinsky tenet,
148; racism/anti-unionism
dressed as, 14, 16, 25, 26, 28 (*see
also* McCarthyism); as Republi-
can right-wing religion, 105
Anzaldua, Gloria, 61, 63
Apples, of Northwest, 8
Apricots, California, 53–54
Arabs, FWA support from Cali-
fornia-based, 43

198

INDEX

39; in Salinas area, 117–20; sit-
down, 29 (see also Sit-ins); in
Texas melon fields, 159–60; of
tomato pickers, 31; UFW deem-
phasis of, 134, 166; by vegetable
workers, 172. See also Sit-ins;
Walkouts
Strikebreakers, 15, 16; braceros as,
29 (see also Bracero Program);
FWA focus on, 43, 45; illegal immigrants as, 8–9, 81, 89, 90,
156–65; Jack London on, 43, 45;
Teamsters as, 54–55, 78, 93, 95,
117–18, 120, 122–23, 126. See also
Goons
Student Nonviolent Coordinating
Committee (SNCC), 48, 57
Students: activism of Chicano, 90;
AFL-CIO incorporation opposed
by, 55; Chávez appeal to elemen-
tary-school, 136; as Chávez sup-
porters, 16, 39, 47–49, 58, 139;
militant, 82, 98, 99, 148, 154;
organization of Chicano, 89; vs.
Vietnam War, 42. See also Movi-
miento Estudiantil Chicano de
Aztlan (MECHA)
Studies on the Left, 97
Sugar beets, California, 12
Supermarkets, picketing of, 16, 91
Swing, Joseph M., 26
Synanon, Chávez debt to, 133, 134

Taft-Hartley Act, 16
Taylor, Ronald, 181, 182
Teacher(s): as Chávez supporters,
26; Huerta as, 66
Teach-ins, campus, 57
Teamsters Union, 182; as company
union, 126; Delano strike support from, 54; farm workers
courted by, 54–55, 57 (see also
Teamsters Union, as strikebreakers); grape grower appeals
to, 92; Nixon deal with, 122; re-
treat of, 131; and Schenley/FWA
negotiations, 53; as strikebreak-

ers, 54–55, 78, 93, 95, 117–18, 120,
122–23, 126; and UFW, 53, 54, 78–
79, 116–18, 120, 122–23, 126, 127,
129, 141, 167, 186. See also Grami,
Bill; Hoffa, Jimmy
Teatro Campesino, El, 48, 152–53,
174, 177; papers of, 187
Tehachapi Mountains, UFW headquarters to, 120
Television: Delano pickets on, 49,
51; violence on, 82
Tenayuca, Emma, 62, 65, 75
Tet offensive, 82
Texas, state of: Chávez campaign-
ing in, 136, 139–41, 155; Chicano
political activism in, 89; Mexican
agricultural workers to, 9, 81;
Mexican American activism in,
76, 89; Mexicans "repatriated"
from, 10; Mexican strikebreakers
in, 159; UFW in, 77–78, 159–60,
180 (see also Nelson, Eugene)
Texas Farm Workers Union, 78
Texas Rangers, 160
Theaters, segregated, 13. See also
Teatro Campesino, El
Thermal, Calif., 42
Thinning, of seedlings, 3, 12
Thoreau, Henry David, 72
Tierra Amarilla, N.M., 83
Tijerina, Reies López, 57–58, 76,
83–84, 139, 141, 143, 149
Tijuana, Mex., 166
Tillich, Paul, 110
Tobacco Workers Union, 14
Toledano, Ralph de, 184
Tomatoes, California, 31
Torres, Art, 134, 173
Tower, John, 160
Training, job: federal commitment
to, 41; Mexican American thirst
for, 145
Translation, as UFW service, 166
Travell, Janet, 89
TreeSweet, 50, 54
Trotsky, Leon, 97
Truth, Chávez veneration of, 108